MADRIGAL SINGING

MADRIGAL SINGING

A Few Remarks on the Study of Madrigal Music with an explanation of the Modes and a Note on their Relation to Polyphony

By CHARLES KENNEDY SCOTT

Second Edition

BOOKS FOR LIBRARIES PRESS
FREEPORT, NEW YORK

Second Edition First Published 1931
Reprinted 1970

STANDARD BOOK NUMBER:
8369-5243-X

LIBRARY OF CONGRESS CATALOG CARD NUMBER:
77-109634

PRINTED IN THE UNITED STATES OF AMERICA

To

THE ORIANA MADRIGAL SOCIETY

FOREWORD

IT is quite impossible to do thorough work in the hour or so every week which is all that most Choral Societies can give to rehearsal. Rough-and-ready methods have to be adopted. Much that should be explained has to be passed over for want of time. The expression is apt to be superficial, stuck on by the conductor, and this sticking on process (to the irritation of both choir and conductor) seems never-ending.

In the matter of expression the choir should at least be able to meet the conductor half-way. To a large extent they should be prepared for what is wanted of them; but ordinary rehearsal is not sufficient for this. It must be done by private study, enthusiastically undertaken by the singers. This is particularly necessary in the case of Madrigal singing; for most choirs are not accustomed to Madrigals, and certain characteristics of Madrigals have to be made clear before they can be sung properly.

I have felt these things very much in connexion with my own Madrigal choir, and it is with the desire of having some little text-book to hand over to the members of the Oriana Madrigal Society that I have put together these few remarks.

I do not think that there is any book, so far, which deals systematically with the singing of polyphonic music, though certain detached articles on the subject are to be found as Prefaces in some of the volumes of Mr. Arkwright's Edition of Old English Music (Joseph Williams). Part of this little work is scarcely more than a paraphrase of these instructive Prefaces, and I should like to admit my obligation to them.

On p. 98 I have added an explanation of the modes and, further on, a Note on Ayres. Every Madrigal singer should know something about the scale system of the music that he is performing. The Note on Ayres has been included chiefly for the purpose of laying stress upon the polyphonic nature of all choral music of the period.

C. K. S.

London, 1907.

And we will sit upon the rocks,
Seeing the Shepherds feed their flocks
By shallow rivers, to whose falls
Melodious birds sing Madrigals.

MARLOWE

CONTENTS

x   *Contents*

MADRIGAL SINGING

Introductory

BY Madrigal singing we mean the performance of all secular choral music composed during the Polyphonic period. The music we shall discuss in the following pages, however, is mainly comprehended between 1588 and 1638.

The word Madrigal is often used in a generic sense. It serves well enough to indicate, collectively, a class of composition where much the same style prevails throughout. But it is necessary to be more precise. There are three main divisions in English Madrigal Music : the Madrigal proper, the Ballet, and the Ayre. Some disagree that the latter falls within the category of Madrigal at all, holding that, in a sense, the Ayre represents principles at variance with the principles of genuine Madrigal composition. It is perhaps possible to maintain that the Ayre in its later presentments by Dowland, Pilkington, and others reflects the new order of monodia, or the single melody principle, rather than the old order of polyphony or the principle of combined melodies which was the feature of Madrigal composition. But we shall try to show later, perhaps by something of special pleading, that the choral Ayre represents the monodic principle in so primitive a form as to leave it scarcely distinguished from the Madrigal in the matter of polyphony: on which score we may still be permitted to classify an Ayre as a Madrigal, and in performance treat it much the same.

The English took little or no part in the development of the Madrigal proper. It must even be admitted that, save in the early days of polyphony, English musicians seldom showed themselves to be innovators in the musical form of either sacred or secular composition.* But when the time came, they none the less proved conclusively that it was not from some national lack of musical instinct that they had failed to establish a progressive school, but that it was from lack of opportunity. Such a time came towards the close of the sixteenth century; too late, indeed, to enable our

---

* 'The forraine artist saith that an Englishman is an excellent imitator, but a very bad inventor; and indeed it should so appeare, for we, observing such inventions which they ensample to us, as Madrigals, Pastoralls, Neapolitans, Ballads and diverse other light Harmonies, do bend our courses only to surpass the tuning of such strings.'—Thomas Ravenscroft, *Apologia* to his *Briefe Discourse*, 1614.

B

English musicians to help in the main work of development, but allowing them a brief period wherein they might show that they could use the Madrigal form with a success in no wise inferior to the success of those who had created and developed it.

Some hundred publications of miscellaneous secular choral music appeared during this period, which may be said to open with Byrd's *Psalmes, Sonets and Songs*, 1588, and to close with Michael Este's *Seventh Set* in 1638. But most of our Madrigals, and certainly the best of them, including those of Wilbye, Benet, Bateson, Gibbons, Kirbye, Morley, Ward, and Weelkes, date between 1595 and 1620.* And the fact that within a quarter of a century our composers produced such store—in so doing opening up a new vein of expression—'the Italian vaine', adapting themselves to what was practically an exotic form, and almost at a bound summing up the possibilities of that form—is a phenomenon unparalleled in musical history

Verse and Music

THE time of our Madrigals was not only the flowering and culmination of one of the greatest periods in music, it was a golden age of poetry as well. Never have musicians been able to dispose of verse so fitted for song; never have poets been served by music so adaptable to verse. Made of nervous, highly varied language, distinguished by imagery and quaint conceit, the Elizabethan lyric stands supreme. Supreme not only for its abundant vitality, but for its full-throated melodiousness. Later poetry often pays little heed to sound. It is intended to be read. But the 'sweet numbers' of Elizabethan verse were assuredly written to be sung.

Strangely enough, we seldom know the authors of the words. A mere handful of madrigalian verse is signed. Of the ninety-four Madrigals of Weelkes, for instance, but two can be identified with the name of a poet. It is only in the case of the Ayres of Thomas Campion that we are on sure ground throughout as to literary origin. And this is due to the quite exceptional fact that he was both a poet and a musician, and set his own words. Thus, given to them to use, much 'immortal verse' owes its preservation to the Madrigal composers and their song books.

* A complete list of the works of our Madrigal writers, printed during their lifetime, is given at the end of this book in an advertisement of the *English Madrigal School*, ed. by Dr. E. H. Fellowes.

The general note of Madrigalian poetry is personal and effusive. It would be grouped under the title of love-poems. Much of it is, as well, pastoral in character, and derives in spirit from Italy; also, in letter, for many of the poems are a direct translation from the Italian, 'brought to speak English'. In which case they are often of second-rate quality.

Renaissance convention of course appears in proper names. These are seldom of the vernacular. Thyrsis and Cloris, Damon and Phyllis, Endymion and Phoebe are the protagonists; scarcely ever Kate and Will, or Jack and Joan. But this does not of itself destroy a truly English note and, when this is given, the words almost always rise to the highest levels of poetic achievement.

Sometimes verse of a moral kind is set, notably by Byrd and Gibbons. 'What is our life', attributed to Sir Walter Raleigh and set by the latter composer, is an example of this. Thus we have not only 'songs of myrth' but 'songs of gravitie'. These latter take us from the livelier main road, into quiet groves of contemplation, and form a most interesting sub-group of madrigalian literature.

Taken generally, verbal movement is much more rapid than musical movement. And it is not pretended that, in 'dittying', the Madrigal composer caused his music to follow a line of rhythm exactly parallel to that of the words. Music has rights and interests of its own, and can never entirely abrogate them in favour of poetry; but it can faithfully follow the essential structure of the words, and indicate their subtly-varied accentuation.

This, Madrigal music did. And though greater emotional resources have, since, been liberated in respect of melody and harmony, in no other vocal music has the utterance of the poet been so safeguarded from formal distortion as in that of the sixteenth century.

To those who are as sensitive to the beauty of words, as of music, the singing of a Madrigal therefore offers an especial satisfaction.

If we try to get at the secret of polyphonic music, one of the first things we shall discover is that its main drift is collective rather than individual. Its nature diffuses the interest over many voices or parts. It does not concentrate it in one. It is typical of the expression of general joy or sorrow, not of a highly passionate, personal outpouring. So that if we are intent on the latter, we shall not turn to a Madrigal. It may even be said that, in this sense, there is often not complete accord between the verse and the music, and that a different musical form would better elucidate the verbal sentiment.

Neither, if we desire a very pronounced throb of physical life, shall we find it in a Madrigal. Animation of the spirit we shall discern in plenty, but it seldom translates itself into periodic pulsation. The snap and stimulus of the dance must be looked for elsewhere. Ballets, of course, do suggest bodily movement, though by no means its full abandon. But the Madrigal, by reason of its structure, cannot do so. Nor, I think, should we expect it, in a general way, from any music allied to poetry. For thought, the stuff of poetry, either in sense or sound, rarely emphasizes a sheerly active element. It has much finer purposes in view. And if the music did so in a song, as it well can, it would be but poorly in accord with poetic imagination. Instruments are the appropriate media for physical expression. And, effectively, we have to go to instrumental forms if we wish for its manifestation. Madrigal music will take us through moods ranging from simple gaiety to profound reflection. But it will neither give us the storm and stress of objective nature, nor even of human nature. It never runs loose. It is sincere, with the ardency of new adventure. But its sincerity is tempered with a certain emotional restraint, inherent in the polyphonic style itself, and due to the comparatively early appearance of medieval polyphony upon the stage of musical development.

Pictorial realistic touches often occur. But qualities of the soul—I had almost said abstract qualities—rather than attributes of the body are its chief revelation. Wanton care-free merriment, a spring freshness—spring is the favourite season of the Madrigalists—pathos, tenderness, and the like are given 'local habitation'. But only so much physical shape as will bring them to earth.

Characteristics of Polyphony and Monodia

A COMPOSITION is polyphonic when all the parts comprising it are melodious and *absolutely equal* in interest.

A composition is monodic when its essence, as it were, is concentrated in one special part, generally the highest; when, in other words, the composition is based upon a single melody.

The supreme sign or mark of polyphony is its imitative character. For the parts of a composition to be equal in interest, each part must show at least distinct and continuous melody. They are incontestably equal in interest when they show not only melody, but the *same* melody, treated in imitative or fugal fashion. The following passage is typical of the imitative polyphonic style :

Lightly she Whipp'd—MUNDAY

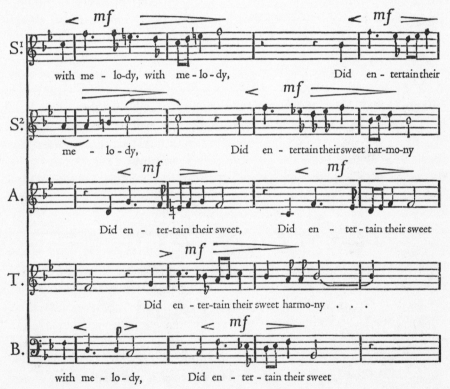

It is here impossible to say that any one voice represents the chief part, for each voice has a similar melody to sing.

But imitation is not necessary for the principles of polyphony to be maintained. In the following passage we cannot determine a principal part :

Sister, Awake—BATESON

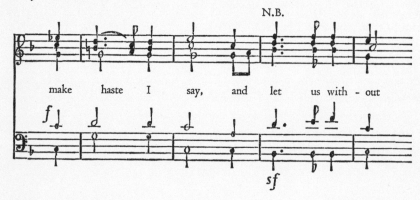

Here each voice is about equally melodious, i.e. the passage is poly-phonic though there is no imitative treatment. Because parts move to-gether, in *coincident* and not *independent* rhythm, it by no means follows that the lower parts are merely harmonizing the melody of the highest part; are in fact subordinate to it. It generally follows in modern music, but not in Elizabethan. In Madrigals the melodic interest is nearly always even and diffused, no matter how the parts are combined as regards rhythm.

Relation of Polyphony to Performance

A KNOWLEDGE of certain characteristics of a Madrigal is indispen-sable to every Madrigal singer. To take up his part intelligently, he must know for what it stands in the economy of the composition. If he is accustomed to modern part-singing, he may perhaps wonder whether his is a principal or a subordinate part; whether he should sing it to the fore as melody or subdue it as accompaniment. He can be told in a few words. There is no such thing as a subordinate part in a Madrigal or in any form of polyphonic music. Even when the voices move mostly note against note, as in the verse sections of Ballets and some of the simpler of the Ayres, it cannot be said that the upper or any one voice is more favoured as regards melody than another. An Ayre or a Ballet shows as unmistakable signs of polyphony as a Madrigal proper. There may not be points of imitation; but the treatment of the parts is distinctly 'horizontal' (to use

Hullah's well-worn simile), i.e. the composition is formed of layers of melody.

In the performance of his part the Madrigal singer has scarcely ever to consider any other part, or to regulate the expression of his part, *in order that some other part may be shown up.* In fact it may be said, as a general rule, that the less attention he pays to what the other parts are doing, the better. In expressing his part well he has sometimes to assert himself a little more than the others, but the others never have to give way to him. When he seems to yield, it is only because his part gives him no opportunity for making it prominent. Take as an extreme instance the first four bars in the Bass part of Dowland's Ayre, 'Awake, Sweet Love'.

Awake, Sweet Love—DOWLAND

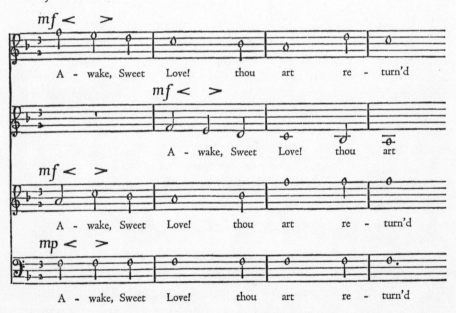

No judicious singer would force these Bass notes. There is no melodic interest in them—this can be seen at a glance—so the good singer will not try to get anything out of them. Hence the part will be automatically subordinated to the melody in the three upper voices. The singer will not sing these F's softly, in comparison, because the three upper voices have the melody. He will do it because he has no melody himself. In a modern part-song it is different. The interest of the piece is largely centred in the highest part, the other parts being clearly marked off for the purpose of mere accompaniment. So that although there may be a certain amount of melodic interest in the subordinate parts, the singer dare not assert it to any great extent, for he knows he is expected to support the melody, not to divert attention from it. In other words, the accompanying parts must be systematically subordinated to the principal part.*

In all kinds of musical performance what is interesting and essential must be brought out; what is poor and unimportant must be subordinated. It is true the parts of a Madrigal may have to be subordinated (as we saw in 'Awake, Sweet Love'); but it is only for the moment. The Madrigal singer *may* have to take a back seat; but he knows that just as often it will be his turn to preside.

In general the interest of a composition is centred in those parts which show relative movement of notes. Parts which remain stationary while the others move are usually but poorly expressive, i.e. unmelodic. Mere repetition of notes does not mean melody. Sometimes, however, a part moving in relatively long notes is important, and must be brought out, as in the well-known passage in the refrain of Weelkes's 'As Vesta was', where the theme in crotchet form is combined with itself in augmented (breve and semibreve) form. Such instances are comparatively infrequent, however; and unless some special point of composition is evident, parts which remain stationary while others move should be somewhat subdued in performance.

* This is a little extreme in statement, but it will serve well enough here.

Melody and Harmony

BOTH polyphonic melody and harmony are of the simplest kind in regard to interval, the latter amounting to little more than play upon common chords, while, underlying the former, is the very practical idea that, since all vocal music has to be imagined before it can be sung, what the mind can easily grasp is likely to be more effectively realized than that which it grasps with difficulty. Thus, difficult intervals are purposely avoided, amongst them, in particular, the tritone F to B, the 'very devil' * in music of those times.*

*Mi contra fa
Diabolus est
In musica.*

In the main, polyphonic melody is diatonic and close knit. If large intervals are used, the part generally returns, filling up the gap, by conjunct motion. A succession of jumps in the same direction is seldom to be met with.

Come, let us rejoice—BYRD

O care, wilt thou despatch me—WEELKES

A characteristic of polyphonic melody, though it weakened towards the end of the polyphonic period, is that it is based upon the old system of modes and not scales. To those unaccustomed to modal melody, many progressions, therefore, may seem strange and even wrong. But close acquaintance brings out a distinction and a flavour that often far surpasses that of progressions written in the more circumscribed range of our modern major and minor scales. This modal treatment, coupled with alteration of the notes according to the laws of *musica ficta*, sometimes engenders harmonic clashes that are apt to disconcert the singer.

Typical passages, in which an F♮ is thrust against an F♯, and vice versa, are shown in the two foregoing examples.

A further example, with pronounced discordance, is from the 'Lullaby' of Byrd (see opposite). The logic of this procedure is of course quite apparent

Lullaby—BYRD

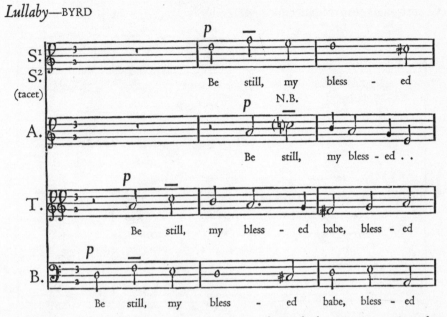

to us now, but up to a few generations ago these clashes were so misunderstood that reputed critics held up their hands in horror at them, and they were 'put to rights', in reprints, by the omission of the offending accidental or otherwise, according to the taste of the time.

It has been said that difficult intervals are avoided in polyphonic music. This rarely needs qualification as regards their use in a phrase; but *between* phrases one interval of even exceptional difficulty, if taken from its context, may occur, viz. that of the diminished 8ve. It is shown in the example below from Ward's Madrigal, 'Hope of my heart', and can be

accounted for in the custom that polyphonic composers had of ending phrases and sections on a major harmony rather than on a minor.* This involved the chromatic alteration of the third of the chord, but, when the cadence was completed, a return was immediately made to the modal note. Hence this particular interval, which may give trouble at first, but s afterwards felt to be natural so that it can be sung with ease.

Rhythm

RHYTHM was defined by Plato as 'order in movement' and by St. Augustine as 'beautiful movement'. Both writers of course had in mind only good rhythm, though obviously there can be bad, disordered movement as well as good. Ordered movement might be roughly classified as (1) verbal and (2) instrumental. It is clear that the former need not be regularly measured. Our everyday speech shows that, though it is quite satisfying in its sweep and balance. But instrumental rhythm, *unsupported by the meaning of words*, must have an easily grasped metrical, or mensurable, basis, which leaves the mind in no doubt as to its logic and structure. 'Sound' meaning is one thing, 'verbal' meaning quite another. The Madrigalists thought that their Madrigals were 'apt for viols and voyces', apparently not realizing this rhythmic distinction; just as, later, it was imagined that instrumental rhythm equally covered vocal rhythm—to a great confusion of styles. Madrigal (and polyphonic) music is certainly not instrumental, though an instrumental style was gradually evolving through it. Its *fons et origo* is the word, which the music 'cloaks', to use an Elizabethan expression. Apart from words its rhythmic form had no *raison d'être*. It was diffuse and pointless. But being bound up with words it could adopt a free or prose rhythm and be quite intelligible, for the words would always give the clue. Mr. Wooldridge has defined polyphonic melody as 'an imaginative mixture of notes', and it was perfectly designed to follow the verbal flow and sensitively adjust itself to it. Thus its rhythm (together with that of plain-song) is the type *par excellence* of verbal rhythm in terms of music. But for the type of instrumental self-supporting rhythm we have to go to the dance, with its regularly recurring periods.

* One of the great charms of polyphonic harmony lies in this convention. Many deliciously unexpected touches arise from it.

Performance of Madrigals as regards Rhythm

IT is one of the attractions of Madrigal singing that each part has more or less the same scope for expression. We must admit this even when the parts move together. Yet it is very much easier to sing a part that moves *with* the other parts, as in the following example:

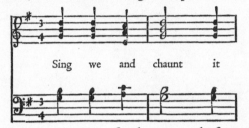

than *against* the other parts, as in a further example from Morley,* where every beat is stressed by one voice or another, though not coincidently.

Round around about a wood—MORLEY

It is this factor of rhythm that largely differentiates the Madrigal proper from the Ballet and Ayre. In the Ayre and Ballet, particularly in the Ballet, the parts will often be found to move together. In the Madrigal, on the other hand, the parts are highly independent. But there are degrees of inde-

---

* Morley—together with his great master, Byrd, 'never without reverence to be named of the musicians'—is one of the most interesting 'practitioners' in rhythmic combinations.

pendence. Three examples will make this clear. For the first, take the eight opening bars of Morley's Ballet, 'My bonny lass'. The rhythm of the first four bars is coincident in every part, so it requires no effort of independence from the singer. In the beginning of the fa-la section there is a certain amount of independent rhythm to be kept. To get precise entries after the rests is a matter of care, but if we show the phrases and accent of each part by the usual signs, it will be seen that the singer's task is comparatively easy.

Ex. 1.

Here the outlines or rhythmic swing of the phrases mostly coincide, as also the accents and expression shape. The first Tenor part differs a little from the second Tenor and Bass by reason of the syncopation, and the accent of the Soprano part at point of entry is stronger than the accent of the under parts, but on the whole this is about the minimum of independence, and does not tax the singer very much more than the coincident rhythm of the first four bars.

A second example shows a greater independence of rhythm :

Ex. 2.   *When shall my Wretched Life*—WILBYE

Here the rhythm only coincides in the Tenor and Bass and the parallel

passage following in the second Soprano and Tenor. All the other parts
work independently.

Such a passage as the above represents a very general level of what is
required rhythmically in singing Madrigals. But the singer must be prepared to go one step further, as in the following :

Ex. 3.   *Thyrsis, sleepest thou*—BENNET

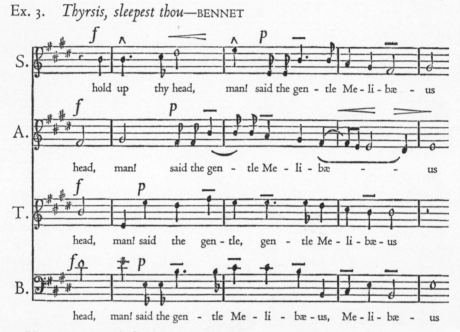

Here it is very difficult to maintain the natural rhythm of the Alto and
Tenor. In our first and second examples it will be seen that most of the
accents fall on the strong beats of the bar, viz. one and three. And although
syncopations have to be dealt with, syncopated accents can always be mentally referred to normal strong beats. Syncopations are only a displacement
of accent from strong beats to weak beats. They do not cancel the prevail-
ing time unless used persistently. But in the Alto and Tenor of our last
example the accents cannot be referred to the strong beats. Although written in duple time, the latter is really in triple time. And this is a great
difficulty for the singer. He gets no support, as in the other cases, from the
regular pulse of the movement. He has to sing against the time, as the
saying goes; and not only this, the other parts are as disconcerting to him

as it is possible for them to be. Their normal accent is actually hostile to the accent which should be given in his part, and it requires a most determined effort to disregard what the other parts are doing.

The Tenor part really stands thus in pronounced triple time :

said the gen - tle, gen - tle Me - li - bæ - us

And the Alto is even of freer and more intricate measure :

man, said the gen - tle Me - li - bæ - - - us

It is not necessary for the singer to imagine such complications of time when he is singing. *It is generally sufficient for him to be guided by the natural accent of the word.* If he is so guided, he will sing such time without knowing it. But he is never absolved from giving the appropriate expression to such passages, no matter how hard it is to secure it. Such a perversion as the following would be intolerable, i.e. keeping the normal accents on the first and third beats:

said the gen - tle, gen - tle Me - li - bæ - us

Though the Alto part is rhythmically more complicated than the Tenor, more care would have to be taken in the expression of the Tenor part, as the notes are nearly all of equal length, and so depend on dynamic accent from the singer for proper effect. But in the Alto part the notes which should be accented are longer than the non-accented notes, and so, even if the singer does not stress them above the rest, they will probably stand out.

This independent expression of a part is the perfection of Madrigal singing, and calls forth the highest qualities of mental control that the singer may possess. The foregoing example from 'Thyrsis' is by no means exceptional. Almost in every Madrigal instances might be shown of this irregular metrical treatment. The rhythm of polyphonic music, in fact, frequently approximates to the 'free', declamatory rhythm of Gregorian chant, where groups of two and three *equal* notes succeed each other in the same rhythmic period. The following example of free rhythm from the chant 'Asperges me' may be interesting as showing this rhythmic similarity:

Plain-song was the ultimate basis of polyphonic music, and this feature of free rhythm is perhaps a survival; but, whether or not, it is evident that polyphonic composers were (1) not bound down to regular metre, and (2) did not trouble when this irregularity was at variance with the time-signature.

It is therefore necessary to observe that, in Madrigal singing, *bar signs should be absolutely disregarded as suggesting accent.* No bar signs are marked in the old part-books.* It was not till about 1650 that the use of bars was established, so that composers were not continually reminded of regular measure and the accent on the first beat that it is generally held to imply. The absence of bar signs might almost be said to have been a direct incentive to free rhythm, or at least permitted it with little sense of incongruity with musical notation.†

Two other examples of this disturbance of normal accent may be added. The following is interesting. It is to be found in the seventeenth of Byrd's *Psalms, Songes and Sonnets,* 1588. He signs the composition in $\frac{3}{2}$ time, and starts off (!) with the following phrase :

---

* Though they are very properly inserted in modern editions of old music.

† Bar signs have perhaps helped to destroy a certain very valuable element of rhythmic freedom and have stereotyped rhythm, in modern music, in a way that often is far from satisfactory. I am not sure whether it would not be better to indicate merely the unit 'stroke' or beat in conducting Madrigals, rather than to group the beats metrically (in threes, fours, &c.). The all-important thing in Madrigal singing is good melodic phrasing, and this might tend to preserve it.

which a modern composer would have written in the totally different rhythm of $\frac{3}{1}$:

If wo - men could be fair and ne - ver fond

This passage from Munday's *Oriana* Madrigal, 'Lightly she whipp'd', may also be quoted :

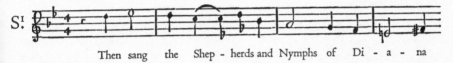

Then sang the Shep - herds and Nymphs of Di - a - na

where two bars of triple time are interspersed in common time. Thus :

Then sang the Shep - herds and Nymphs of Di - a - na

To pass on to another point. A frequent habit of the polyphonic writers was, in triple time, to subdivide the beats so that either simple or compound time resulted. Thus in Byrd's 4-part Madrigal, 'This sweet and merry month', we find :

for plea - sure of the joy - ful time

in which the second bar is, of course, really in compound $\frac{6}{4}$ time and must be interpreted as such. Madrigal singers must immediately be up to this shifting of the accentual structure, which is apt to be very confusing unless a considerable discipline has prepared them for it. What they will feel like doing is to sing the phrase thus :

instead of spacing this second duple bar over *three* beats.

It is not enough, either, to look upon the passage as of a syncopated nature in simple triple time, thus :

The full flavour of it can only be disengaged if it is felt as a compound time with two *direct* accents.

When all the voices are coincident as in the foregoing, this rhythmic peculiarity is exhibited in its simplest form. But composers, particularly Byrd, also delighted in contrasting the voices, so that one should be singing in simple while another had compound time, e.g. :

Though Amaryllis dance—BYRD

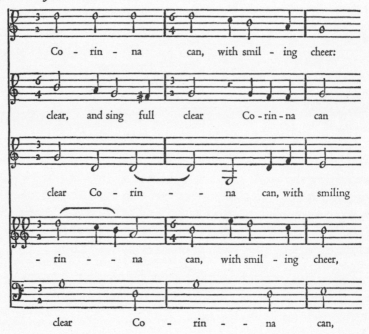

This is exceedingly confusing to the singer, and to be able to perform it well, both individually and collectively, represents perhaps the *ne plus ultra* of rhythmic accomplishment.

It is only occasionally that the proportion of $3 = 2$ has to be nego-tiated in Madrigal singing. Curiously enough, it is much oftener to be met with in modern than in polyphonic music, and it is of course far easier to sing than a combination of $\frac{3}{2}$ and $\frac{6}{4}$, because in it the first note of each group coincides. A comparatively rare instance of this *sesquialtera* propor-tional treatment, as it was termed, is to be found in another Psalm by the endlessly inventive Byrd :

Make ye joy to God

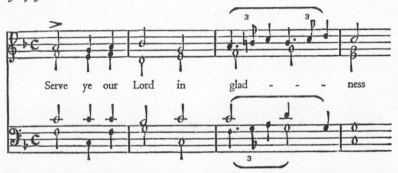

Here it may well be asked how, in a Madrigal, does metre come in at all? Why should the composer put a time-signature to his music, as he does, if he never keeps to it nor expects the singer to keep to it? The answer is, that though there is (or may be) no accentual regularity in the individual parts of a polyphonic composition, yet there is a sort of metrical basis underlying the work as a whole. In broad terms it may be said that the horizontal melodic element is free, but that the vertical harmonic ele-ment is regularly measured. And as harmonies are built upon a bass, it will be the *bass* which will for the most part determine the general rhythm.

Thus a Bass such as this, from another of Byrd's Psalms :

could not be referred to anything but duple time; but the next phrase:

though noted in C time, can readily be taken as :

Regular metrical treatment can always be relied upon in cadences, where suspensions are usually involved and have a fixed treatment as regards accent, but apart from the cadence the singer will often come across a good deal of ambiguous, and even fictitious, metrical notation, not only in the individual voices, but the general sense of the music.

A very striking passage from the same Psalm is :

Arise, Lord, into Thy rest—BYRD

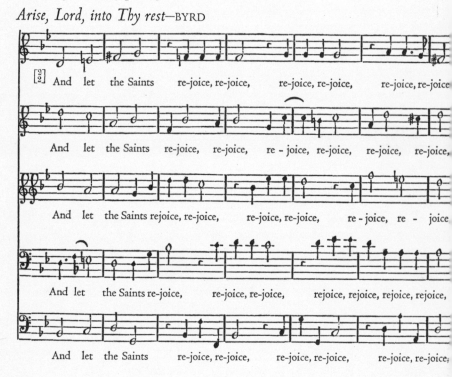

This, though written in duple time, in reality encloses a quite clear and constant triple time, and should be barred thus, with a signature of $\frac{3}{2}$:

We also see here groupings of $\frac{3}{2}$ and $\frac{6}{4}$ combined with astonishing ingenuity and symmetrical beauty. The $\frac{6}{4}$ is, of course, in the second soprano part, which in the original duple time notation, it will be observed, was much syncopated. It may be said here that syncopations are very often signs of duple giving way to triple measure, though there is no indication of it in the time-signature. The singer should therefore always be on the alert as to what is involved in a syncopation.

The reverse case of a longish passage being noted in triple time but having the sense of duple is harder to find. A bar or two of it, however, is often met with, as in Byrd's 'Carol for Christmas Day', which has :

and the same treatment is applied to cadences as a very favourite device, continued long after the polyphonic period by Purcell and Handel, such as in the following, where bars 4 and 5 (together) undoubtedly give a sense of $\frac{3}{1}$:

Sing ye to our Lord—BYRD

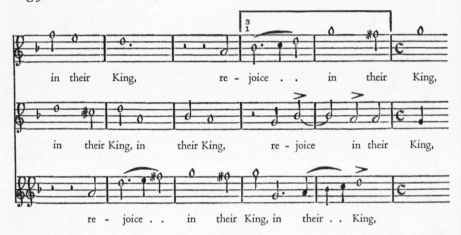

It will be seen that these last two examples are merely a variant of the same principle that underlies our previous 'For pleasure' example, viz. the use of triple measure to cover, it may be, either a simple or compound time. Here the process occurs over *two* bars instead of one, that is all.

It may be said that, in general, duple time served the composer for freer metrical treatment than did triple time, and it was the time that most readily sheltered irregular twos and threes. When triple time is used in polyphony it is mostly in passages of pronounced metrical lilt, and its signification must be taken as altogether more precise than duple time.

To sum up—though metre has been discussed at some little length in this section—our main object has been to persuade the singer that his individual part may be, and mostly is, unmetrical; and that the cue to right accenting should be always the word and never the bar-line. This is the great lesson he has to learn.

The Expression of Dissonance

THE proper expression of a Madrigal is achieved almost entirely by singing the separate melodies well. It is nearly independent of any harmonic consideration. The principle of harmony exists in a Madrigal, but it is worked out through melody. We saw this even in the case of the extreme discords noted on pp. 9, 10, and 11.* That is to say, to the Madrigal composer harmony was not a first consideration, but a secondary one, something which was involved by the simultaneous combination of melodies. This being the case, it would seem as if we had no need to dwell on dissonance which is a feature of harmony. But we propose to discuss Madrigal dissonance somewhat, not because it directly affects Madrigal singing to any extent, but because it may be seen how necessary proper melodic expression is, if the features of a Madrigal (which include the feature of dissonance) are to be made clear.

Parts may be either consonant or dissonant to one another. Parts are consonant to each other at any fixed point when they give an impression of rest or completeness; they are dissonant when they give the effect of incompleteness, when they require to proceed one step further, as it were, to produce repose. This step further is called the resolution of the dissonance.

Consonance and dissonance are perhaps best explained by examples already given.

In example 1 the parts are entirely consonant. In 2 there are two dissonances each marked by an asterisk. In the fourth bar is seen the dissonance

---

* The appeal of a Madrigal is almost entirely through melody. It is different with music of a later date, after harmony became a detached principle and was cultivated for its own sake. The bare harmonic scheme of a movement of a Beethoven Sonata can stand by itself as coherent and even interesting. Provided there is a certain accuracy, the performance of a modern choral piece will always give some good effect. It may not bring out the melody of the parts; but it will delineate the harmony, and from this some satisfaction may be derived. But, with a Madrigal, no such satisfaction can be had from the harmony, as harmony. It is true that in a Madrigal the various melodies combine to form harmony; but the resultant harmony is insufficient to interest of its own account, largely because the composer does not present it in clear, self-sufficing rhythmic form—not because it is unvaried or monotonous. Without the saving grace of good melodic expression a Madrigal is almost meaningless, and this is probably why the performance of Madrigals and such-like so often fails to convince. People cannot be bothered with polyphonic music when they only hear it in this way; and they are quite right.

of the seventh from the Bass ; in the fifth bar that of the fourth from the Bass.* In the former the seventh (D) resolves on the sixth (C): in the latter the fourth (A) resolves on the third (G♯).

Ex. 1. CONSONANCE—MORLEY

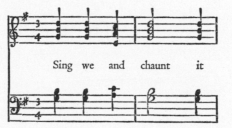

Ex. 2. DISSONANCE—WILBYE

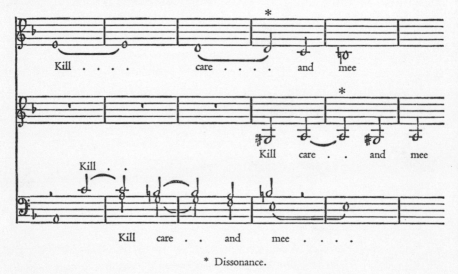

* Dissonance.

In Madrigal music these dissonances are always *prepared*, i.e. the dissonant note has been heard in the same part immediately before, as a consonance. Whence these discords are called discords by prolongation or suspension. The formula of a Madrigal discord is therefore as follows :

* These are the principal Madrigal dissonances ; but sometimes the ninth is suspended.

* Preparation of dissonance.
† Suspension of note as a dissonance.
‡ Resolution of dissonance.

Dissonance plays a very important part in music. It has always been recognized that the expressive power of music resides largely in the use of dissonance, and the development of musical expression has proceeded, perhaps, more on the lines of the emancipation of dissonance than anything else. Morley, in giving rules to be observed in dittying (i.e. setting words to music), says in his *Plaine and Easie Introduction to Practicall Musicke*, 1597: 'You may also use cadences bound with the fourth or seventh, which being in long notes, will exasperate the harmonies,' from which I think we may understand that he regarded dissonance as a disturbing element in music. At any rate, whatever he means, we find it applied accordingly in Madrigal music. With their keen sense of fitness the Elizabethan composers only used 'exasperated' harmony when exasperated treatment was required or, in other words, at times of emotional disturbance, when they wished to express 'complaint, dolour, repentance, sighs, tears and such like'. They rarely used dissonance in Ballets or when dealing with light-hearted, frolicsome subjects. Thus in Wilbye's six-part Madrigal, 'When shall my wretched life', where the music strains towards the expression of plight and anguish, we find that forty out of eighty-five bars, or roughly a half, contain dissonance, whereas in Morley's Ballet, 'Sing we and chaunt it', only two out of twenty-three bars are so treated, or ten out of sixty-seven bars in Bateson's joyous Madrigal, 'Sister, awake'.

The use of dissonance is, therefore, well defined in Madrigal music ; and, inasmuch as only the comparatively mild form of discord by suspension is used, we must make the most of these discords as expressive features.

In a consonant chord the relationship of the notes is comparatively simple. In a dissonant chord it is more complicated. Hence dissonances must be forced upon the ear, so to speak, in order that the ear may understand them.* The dissonant note must stand out from the other parts though not unduly.† This will nearly always be brought about of itself, *if the melodies* (which induce the dissonance) *are well sung.* For these dissonances very frequently occur at some point where a melodic accent is required, independent of any harmonic consideration, i.e. at the climax of a phrase, &c.

The example from Wilbye, previously quoted, will make this clear.

Ex. 1.

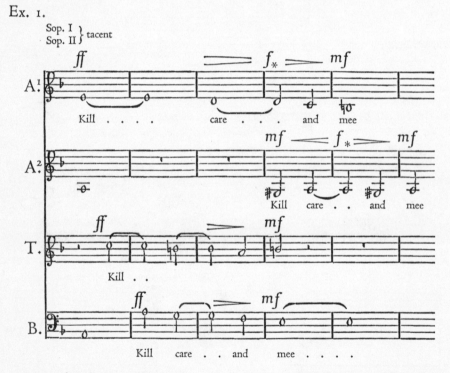

Here the climax of each phrase is on the word 'care', and if this word

---

* This is the case with all striking and exceptional features in music, such as chromatic notes, &c.

† Madrigal dissonances are little more than artificial variations of consonances, so they do not need that violent treatment that must often be given to modern percussive, i.e. unprepared, dissonance.

is accented and followed by an appropriate *diminuendo*, the dissonance at * in the first and second Alto will naturally become prominent.

A still more simple example may be given from Morley's Ballet, 'Fire, fire' :

Ex. 2.

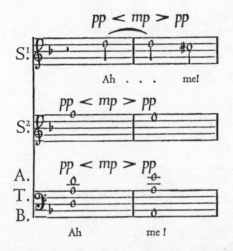

Here the first Soprano has the dissonance, and the swell appropriate at the exclamation 'ah', if indulged in by all the voices, will still clearly show the expression of the dissonance in the first Soprano.‡

‡ The 'swell' here is also appropriate because of a certain eager, urgent quality inherent in a discord by suspension. It is as if the dissonant note had been left behind and strives to catch up to its proper place. One should distinguish these accents of prolongation from syncopated or displaced accent, which, as it were, works backwards instead of forwards. Such a passage as

really stands for

and the dissonance at the *sforzando* is produced by forcing the lower parts against the top part, not by trailing the top part over the others. In other words, the dissonance in the first case comes from the progress of the dissonant part itself ; in the second case, from the 'back-kick' of the

In the foregoing examples it will be seen that the singer is guided simply by the principles of melodic expression; by the length and position of the dissonant note in the melodic phrase. No knowledge of harmony is required in such cases as these (and, as before observed, they constitute the majority). The singer does not even need to know that he is singing a dissonance. But sometimes he is required to know, when the dissonance is not in the shape of a syncopated (long) note as in the following example :

Ex. 3. *Thus saith my Chloris*—WILBYE

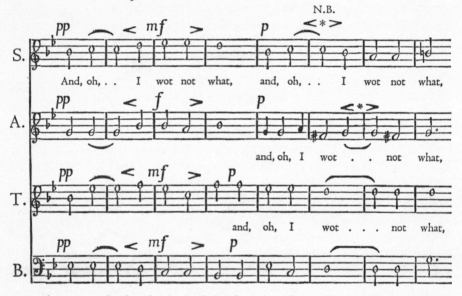

In this example the rhythm of the first four bars is coincident in all the parts, and all the parts rise to an accented climax at the word 'wot'. In bar three the Alto B♭ is the dissonant note; but from a melodic point of view there is nothing to make this B♭ more accented than, say, the Soprano E♭. These notes constitute the highest point in both phrases, and their length is the same. Nevertheless, because of its dissonant character the B♭* must be sung more emphatically than the notes at the same place in the other

accompanying parts. This sort of 'jazz' accent is seldom if ever met with in polyphonic music, which is distinguished above all by a beautiful forward flow—one might almost say—of *serene* movement.

* It should be remarked that this dissonant B flat is, in reality, the same form of dissonance as in the preceding examples. It is prepared in the preceding bar, but is not *tied* to its preparation.

parts. For melodic reasons slight swells should be made on the Sop. C in bar five, and the Alto G in bar six : so both these dissonances (marked *) will be rendered apparent.

As to the dissonances referred to under the heading 'Melody and Harmony', these must not be shirked or watered down by tentative handling. There is no need to apologize for them. Rather should they be gloried in, as points of colour, though treated without exaggeration. In the first Byrd example, on p. 9, a swell on the word 'joy' is quite appropriate, which will thrust the F♮ against the F♯ in an attempt at friendly agreement, so to speak; but as this cannot be satisfied, it accepts the rebuff and retires. In the Weelkes example, the F♯ should be strongly emphasized with a sharp upward sense, and the F♮ should be held firmly so as to come to grips with it—a course fully justified melodically by the importance of the word 'deadly' and also in order to make the anguished harmonic point that the composer intended. The emotional background of the Byrd 'Lullaby' is the Mother's apprehension lest the infant Saviour King may share the fate of the other Innocents, and this particular harmonic treatment helps to show her unrest. But no special effect of emphasis is required to bring this out. The natural flow of the vocal parts, with a slight underlining of the word 'still', will do all that is wanted, after the manner indicated.

To sum up, Madrigal dissonance nearly always expresses itself *automatically* (as in examples 1 and 2). In comparatively few cases is a knowledge of harmony needed (as in example 3). Yet a knowledge of harmony (which includes the power of being able to locate dissonances) is very valuable as a sort of second string to good melodic expression. For if the nature of the melody is not sufficient to suggest the proper accent and nuances to the singer, he may be stimulated to make the proper expression because he knows that he has to deal with a dissonance. To say the least, a knowledge of harmony is liable to make the Madrigal singer infinitely more careful of his expression; for he then realizes more fully how dependent the expression of the whole Madrigal is on the separately perfect expression of each vocal part.

If the singer were reading from the old part-books, he could never tell at sight whether he were dealing with a dissonance or not; but this is one of the disadvantages of the method of printing separate parts of a composition.

Accent of Chord on Minor 7th

THE use of a Flat to correct the modes often gives rise to a particular chord progression which calls for special accent. The following is an example:

Ex. 1. *Those dainty Daffadillies*—MORLEY

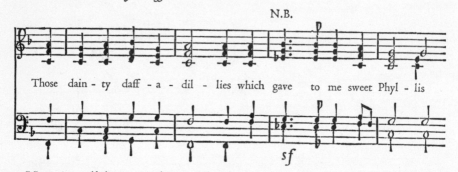

Those dain - ty daff - a - dil - lies which gave to me sweet Phyl - lis

Here it will be seen that in the fourth bar the natural note E of the mode is flattened. If the minor 7th from the final was not available in the mode in which he wrote, the polyphonic composer deliberately flattened the major 7th of the mode to avoid the unsatisfactory chord of the diminished 5th. He scarcely ever tolerated a common chord on what we should term the leading note of a scale, and from this is due some of the peculiar dignity of polyphonic music.

Ex. 2. *Sister, awake*—BATESON

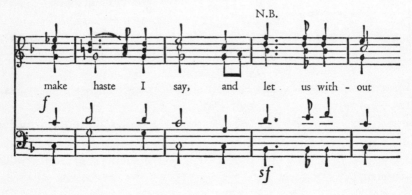

make haste I say, and let us with - out

The example from Bateson (p. 32) amounts to practically the same thing as the Morley example. In the Byrd example there is a sort of appoggiatura treatment of the chord on the minor 7th, and in the Bennet example (after the close in E major) the chord on the minor 7th (of E major) serves to bring a return to the original key.

The reasons why this chord should be specially accented are easily explained on the principle of what is strange and abrupt requiring more emphasis than what is regular and connected.

Ex. 3. *Come, let us rejoice*—BYRD

Ex. 4. *All creatures now*—BENNET

Chords are related to one another in proportion as they have common notes, that is to say, the major chord of C is very akin to that of the minor chord on A because of the common notes C and E; and the passage from one to the other is smooth in consequence; similarly, in lesser degree, from the chord of C major to the chord of F or G major because of the common note between them. But in the progression, as in example 1, from the chord of F major to that of E♭ major there is no such relationship, and hence the greater difficulty of accepting the former chord, i.e. it must be impressed more forcibly on the ear, or, in other words, accent must be given to it.

A still more weighty reason for underlining the chord is that it appears 'out of key' especially to those ears trained to the effect of our modern scales.

In example 4 the *pp* instead of *sf* will be noted at the change of chord, but sudden *pp* is here equivalent to an accent, by contrast, and may often be used with fine effect in such cases.

It should be added that sometimes the Madrigal composer undoubtedly intended to use this chord in an expressive sense. Thus, in the following passage :

Thyrsis, sleepest thou?—EAST

the woeful character of the chord serves to give significance to the word 'all', and an accent or swell is very appropriate upon it.

Accent on Chromatic Notes

ACCIDENTALS are chiefly used in Madrigals to correct the natural notes of the modes in cadences, and also to correct the interval of the tritone, e.g. F♮ to B♮, or the diminished 5th, e.g. E♮ to B♭ (whether the notes occur consecutively as melodic notes, or simultaneously as harmonic notes). But sometimes, during the course of a phrase, accidentals are used for what are distinctly purposes of colour.* Such chromatic notes should be underlined. Example :

Happy, oh, happy he—WILBYE

Here the B♮ in the Treble was evidently inspired by the word 'weary', and lends beautiful pathos to the concluding strain of the Madrigal.

* Morley in his *Plaine and Easie Introduction to Practicall Musicke*, 1597, speaks of natural and chromatic notes in this fashion: 'The natural motions are those which are naturally made betwixt the keyes, without the mixture of any accidentall signe or cord, bee it either flat or sharpe : and these motions be more masculine, causing in the song more virilitie than those accidentall cords which are marked with these signes ♯ ♭ which be indeede accidentall, and make the song as it were more effiminate and languishing than the other motions, which make the song rude and sounding : so that those naturall motions may serve to expresse those effects of cruelty, tyrannie, bitterness, and such others : and those accidentall motions fitly expresse the passions of griefe, weeping, sighes, sorrowes, sobs, and such like.'

Special Progressions

A PROGRESSION specially characteristic of Wilbye is :

Come, Shepherd Swains—WILBYE

where the Bass, at its lowest point, descends to a very expressive note and combines with the other parts to make an accent suggestive of deep poignant emotion. The Madrigal composers also gained very expressive effects by making the voices converge on to the second inversion of the *major* common chord—Bateson particularly, as in the example 'Down the Hills Corinna Trips' (p. 37).

In Ward's 'Hope of my Heart' there is also another good example, somewhat different to the Bateson example in that the chord is approached differently.

Accent is always provoked on the 4th and 6th whenever this chord occurs ; but especially on the 6th (the F sharp, Tenor, in the Bateson ex., and the Alto F sharp in the Ward ex.), which is the characteristic note.

Down the Hills Corinna Trips—BATESON

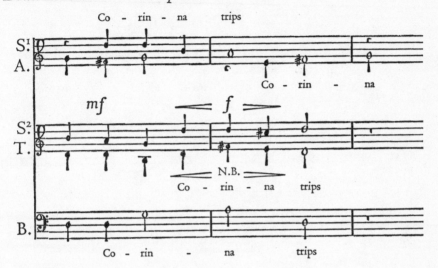

Hope of my Heart—WARD

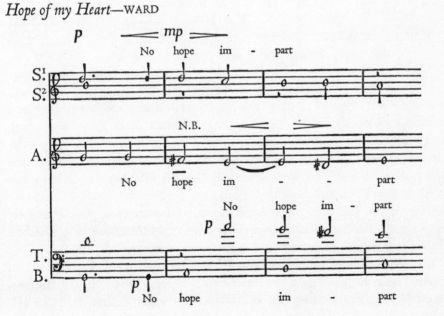

Voice Production

PART singing is the supreme test of vocal excellence. Faults of tone and frailties of technique, which might pass unnoticed in a solo, show up astonishingly under conditions where the onus of expression lies entirely on the singer, and both blend and effectiveness are required.

It is sometimes supposed that any voice is good enough for chorus singing. That a good voice is merely wasted in a chorus. That voices which one would dread to hear separately become very fine in combination. It may be so—under conditions when really nothing matters very much; when the size of a choir, the accompaniment of a big orchestra, the music which is sung, or the place where it is sung, make beauty and refinement an impossibility. Under such conditions individual defects of voice *may* disappear in a chorus; but there can be no high standard of choral singing, and particularly of Madrigal singing, unless the members of the choir can give a good account of themselves separately, as well as sing in combination. A Madrigal singer *should* be a solo singer—and something more.

A good voice depends upon (1) the management of the breath; (2) the freedom of the vocal mechanism; (3) the delivery of the sound.

Breath should be ample and taken largely at the base of the lungs, without raising the shoulders. It should be controlled so that there is no leakage; so that only so much breath is used as is required for the vocal tone. Deep breathing braces the physique, clears the intellect, and heightens feeling. Few realize the enormous potencies that lie in a full use of the breath; that in the development or neglect of its resources lie strength or weakness; that will-power and breath-control are almost one and the same thing.

What may be called the 'locking' of the vocal mechanism—so that the breath, larynx, and resonance chambers function together, and are, so to speak, 'in gear'—also depends upon a full breath. Both figuratively and in effect the voice is a broken reed if its mechanism is disjointed.

The ideal of freedom in singing should be that of 'liberty in law'.

The fetish of 'looseness' is responsible for many undeveloped and in-effective voices, and also for a lack of rhythmic vitality and general alertness. For special effects of *mezza voce* and the like there has to be a certain localized looseness, but complete looseness would mean complete loss of tone. It may seem that if the voice is not loose it must be stiff, rigid, tied-up. But this does not follow. The thread of sound has to be twisted tight, just as a thread of cotton, if it is to have any strength; and so the normal condition of the vocal apparatus should be taut, but at the same time elastic; having spring but yet resistance. A violinist would get no tone if his bow arm were flabby and if his violin were not held firmly against it; and in proportion as he can 'grit' the bow on the resisting string, with perfect control and regularity, so he has fine tone. The good violinist will get much more sound with much less bow expenditure than a bad violinist, and it is the same with a singer. The good singer will get much more tone with much less breath, than the bad one. But only if the condition of elastic tautness is preserved.

The great thing in singing, as in all human endeavour worth having, is concentration: the gathering together of the whole physical and spiritual system so that it is focused on the work in hand, and hence operates with the maximum effect. If the singer can recall a situation in which he has had a great fright, or imagine the tense apprehension which he might experience, say, if confronted by a ghost, he will realize how, in exceptional conditions, often allied with self-preservation, absolute concentration takes place. And it is not too much to assert that a similar almost spell-bound concentration must be present in singing, and particularly in ensemble singing, where the performer has to fit in with an interpretative scheme not entirely of his own making, and instantaneous reaction in the matter of leads, rhythm, and expression is required.

But beware of getting 'tied up' with deep breathing, of becoming rigid. Even virtue has its dangers.

When you have to breathe, recover quickly. If the chest is kept expanded all the time, this will be quite easy. Do not heave the chest with each breath, or let it collapse to expel the breath. Breath must be expelled by pressure from below, so that the voice is *lifted* upon it; or rather the voice should as it were lie *floating* upon the breath, in perfect poise and balance. This is the counterpart of *rapture* on the spiritual side, and music is a poor thing without it.

It should be possible, by good breathing, to sustain notes in all shades of tone and throughout the whole range of the voice without the slightest wavering. Tremulous, unsteady voices mean uncertain harmonies. In an ascending passage breath-pressure should never be relaxed. *If the voice rises, there should always be a feeling of increase in pressure.* The level (or depth) of the breath varies a good deal according to the quality and pitch of the tone; but, allowing for this, it is well to have the breath-effort as low as possible, or, in other words, as far off the larynx as possible, so that the throat may be open and unconstrained.

For the series of vowels ah . . . oo the tongue should lie flat, or even a little concave, in the pit of the mouth. Bad singing is usually throaty or nasal. Both these faults are from undue contraction of the vocal mechanism. If the voice is tight, it can usually be freed by aspirating it a little; mixing an 'h' with the sound. 'H' is the loosener.

A 'forward' production should be cultivated. The aim should be to concentrate the voice and direct it towards the hard palate just behind the teeth, from where it is best reflected *outwards*. Try to 'send' your voice as far as you can; with point and precision, like a shot from a modern rifle. The simile seems to have an unmusical 'crack', but in reality it is apt. As much force was used in the old blunderbuss as in a firearm of to-day, but the result was very different. The former was ineffective, because the force was ill-controlled, ill-directed; it was a purposeless expenditure of energy. The voice may be just as ineffective as a charge from an old blunderbuss, unless the mind and intelligence control it to the desired end. To smother your audience with sound is one thing; to pierce its heart, its emotions, another.

In general the voice should be bright and clear. Notes easily become cloudy. They require to be clarified, like wine.

Vitalize the sound, by continuous breath play upon it, from start to finish. A sustained sound is not necessarily a *living* sound. A living sound is one which you feel throughout.

The question of the registers should solve itself by good breathing, freedom from rigidity and forward production. But, in chorus singing, it

may be necessary to see that Altos do not go above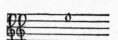

in the chest voice; that Tenors 'close' on and above

that Basses begin to 'cover' about

Of the above, that which relates to Tenors is the most important, as an 'open' quality of voice above the note indicated tends to a sort of shout which refuses to blend with the rest of the voices. Which is just another way of saying that, at all times, the voice must be deeply rooted in the breath.

The mouth should not merely hang in a more or less stupid fashion. It is an instrument to work with.

Beautiful performance comes perhaps most of all from the 'touch' on notes : the sensitive, controlled way in which they are attacked.

A hard 'core' should exist in every note, though its outward appearance may be wonderfully soft and sympathetic.

Learn to distinguish between intensity and loudness. Get the greatest meaning from the smallest amount of tone.

Sing easily and fluently. Be able to pass from one note to another without apparent effort.

Sostenuto is inseparable from rapidity; otherwise there will be a mere spit of breath, instead of tone, in quick notes.

Don't hack out the notes; mould them.

A voice is made; not born.

Vowels

CONSONANT utterance especially gives the measure of vitality in singing; but loveliness is rather with the vowels.

Differentiate the vowels as much as you can. In English there are thirty and more which need to be defined. This means vigorous use of the mouth, for it is largely by the shape of the mouth that vowel difference is secured. Mind 'Oo' and 'Oh', the most deeply expressive vowels we have, and which therefore cannot be adequately sung with shallow feeling. It should be sheer delight to model such a word as 'roses', with its soft, full body-tone, that can be tinted and coloured like the flowers themselves.

The pronunciation of the long close vowels 'Ee' and 'Oo' should not be altered when they have to be sung on high notes; nor, indeed, should any vowel be altered because of pitch.

Pay special attention to the short vowels, which are so characteristic of the English language. Being short, in speech, as their name implies, we are unaccustomed to sustain them, and when, in song, we may have to do so, are apt to modify their pronunciation towards that of the long vowels.

The short i as in 'hit', the long Ee as in 'heat' should be kept quite distinct, similarly the vowels in 'met' and 'mate', 'fatter' and 'father', 'cot' and 'caught', 'dull' and 'dole', 'full' and 'fool'. It is of great importance to have command over the short vowels for two reasons: not only that words in which they occur may be perfectly recognizable, but because, having in a special degree the quality of 'forward' production, they set the whole style of singing in that direction. It is a good plan, indeed, in voice training to consider the long vowels as extensions of the short, so that all the point and brightness of the latter may be retained throughout.

'He clears his voice with a sip of the dew' was written of the blackbird's song. Nothing clears the human voice like practice in the short vowels, and all the *desiderata* of fine singing, economy of sound, brilliancy of tone, keen diction, and much else, are stimulated by it.

The sentence which includes the short vowels, and is given as a mnemonic aid to shorthand, 'That pen is not much good,' should always be remembered; and it should be spoken till it can be brought right on the lips, teeth, and fore part of the face. Then, as a further exercise, in order to get the right position of these vowels, each may be articulated on a single note, several times, with a closed glottis attack, thus:

Finally, a little phrase, such as:

can be sung to the sentence, in ascending keys.

Stress has been laid on the short vowels, for experience has shown that most voices are deficient in their particular quality. But, in a sense, they are only the starting-point for good tone, not the end. Taken by themselves they are not capable of any great expression, which only occurs with the richness and depth of the long vowels. Our main concern here has been to suggest that short-vowel quality should never be *subtracted* from long-vowel quality, except for very occasional colour; though it is quite right and proper to *add* long-vowel quality to that of the short.

'I', as in 'sigh', with no trace of 'Ah' or 'Aw' in it, yet free and sonorous, is perhaps the hardest vowel to manage.

The need for *sostenuto* in singing will be stressed later, but here it may be said that notes should not only be sustained, they should, for foundational work, be of even weight. There would be no difficulty in this if the same vowels were concerned throughout, but there is a great difficulty when, in connexion with words, the vowel is constantly changing. An 'Ee' will be thin and piercing, an 'Oo' feeble, or an 'Ah' will boom out of the picture. There will be no unity in the vocal stream. It will be a series of unrelated blobs. Try therefore to get what amounts to the same power and weight in all vowels. A simple chorale or hymn with one note to each syllable affords perhaps the best test (and practice) of this. Herein your sin will immediately find you out. Scarcely anything is so difficult to sing well as a hymn.

Quality of Tone

MADRIGALS are generally of a light type of fancy, and so weighty tone is not appropriate to their expression. Basses and Contraltos will often be found to err in the tone they use, for this kind of voice is usually thick and backward;* but indeed all voices in Madrigal singing should pay special attention to keeping the voice well forward and avoiding too much neck resonance. The settled pompousness of a heavy voice

* The French say that the English 'swallow their words'; and Milton remarks upon much the same thing in the following quaint passage from his *Essay on Education*, wherein he says that the pupils' speech is to be fashioned to a distinct and clear pronunciation, as near as may be to the Italian, especially in the vowels. 'For we Englishmen, being far northerly, do not open our mouths in the cold air wide enough to grace a southern tongue, but are observed by all other nations to speak exceeding close and inward. . . .'

has little in common with the airy freedom of a Madrigal, nor will it delineate a Madrigal on the purely musical side.

An ideal note may be likened to a pyramid, and it is not entirely fanciful to consider the tip of the nose as the point of the pyramid, from which the note opens *downwards* in ever-increasing volume. The more eloquent the sound, the more broadly it is based on the breath. But, obviously, the grandest sonorities must be reserved for exceptional moments.

For Madrigals there is perhaps less occasion to use what may be called full-scale tone, than for music of a later date. The typical Handelian chorus, for instance, or indeed almost any orchestrally accompanied chorus, is of altogether more weighty pronouncement than a Madrigal, which even in a passionate outburst is distinguished by a certain refinement and reticence, and relies on intensity rather than on power for its effects. Therefore a heavier-lined tone is more appropriate to the one than to the other.

But what *is* wanted for Madrigals is tone in which reedy, nasal resonance has full play. Linear clearness, the most important thing in Madrigal expression, cannot be secured without it. Hence our previous insistence on the value of the short vowels. 'Covered' tone—certainly the extremes of it, when unduly thick and sombre—has no penetrative or 'outstanding' quality, and is really an effaced tone from which beautiful effects of harmonic blend or accompaniment may be secured, but at the expense of the individuality of the component notes, which will tend to disappear in the mass. Thus, if individual notes cannot be detected, it will be likewise impossible to follow the melodic line, which includes them.

Two warnings, however, may be given here. First, there is a bad as well as a good nasal tone. The good seems quite natural and effortless; the bad seems unnatural, and draws attention to itself because it is a deformed tone. In the one the tone freely enters the nasal cavities; in the other it cannot, because the soft palate is contracted. So that what we usually associate with an American or Cockney twang and call nasal tone is, paradoxically, caused by an absence of nasality, not the reverse.

The second warning relates to 'whiteness' of tone, and here again two sorts of whiteness must be indicated. The one, devoid of meaning, and due to merely superficial singing; the other a radiant burning whiteness, in which, so to speak, the whole vocal being is aflame and the full brilliancy of the voice is manifest. Such a whiteness, which is closely related to good nasality, should represent the normal singing tone, from which all modification should come.*

This modification is essential to the complete art of singing. Good normal tone is not enough. It is the imaginative application of good tone, in all its varied colour, that shows the real temper of the singer. Vowels may be looked upon as colours. You may have to brighten or shade them. This is analogous to the play of sunlight on visual colour. Colours alter a great deal according as the weather is bright or dull, and vowels alter also, according as they express feeling which is grave or gay. For happy, sunlit tone you must have a smiling countenance, a high, eager, buoyant breath; for tone which is to interpret sadness, depth of feeling, nobility, &c., you must have a serious countenance, a rounded mouth, and a low breath.

There must be a feeling of resistance in every note. No note should *escape* from the singer, nor go through the nose. It should be held at the nose by a certain muscular effort, which is linked up with breath-effort and is as it were a pull-back of the tone.

Articulation

SINGING, in a sense, is idealized declamation. Whenever possible 'sing as you would speak', placing more stress on important words (nouns, verbs, and particularly on qualifying adjectives and adverbs) than on unimportant words (articles, prepositions, &c.). In quick music this can nearly always be done, though slow, expressive compositions do not admit of it in the same degree.

Articulate clearly. Make your words intelligible, so that the listener knows exactly what you are trying to say and sing. This means pure vowels and splendidly distinct consonants. In singing, as compared with speech, vowels are greatly prolonged; so that unless the consonants are exaggerated, both in strength and generally in length, words are entirely overbalanced in favour of the vowels, and become unrecognizable. The sung word, in short, must be the spoken word raised to a higher power, alike as regards

* Philosophically considered, dark tone is really bright tone modified. No light can come from darkness, though, like virtue, it can be dimmed or even wholly eclipsed. And just as most people have some original sin about them which needs eradicating, so natural, untrained voices are seldom as clear as they should be owing to faulty production, and a bright ringing tone has generally to be acquired.

consonant and vowel. If your words are *not* clear, it means that *you* are mentally fuddled; if they are clear, it means that you *understand* what you are singing about. Eloquent words are the chief end of all good singing.

Good articulation is not only necessary for the sense of the words to be made clear (and of what use are words unless to convey sense?), but it also contributes to the production of good tone by loosening the vocal mechanism. The impulse derived from well-articulated consonants adds life and brilliancy to the voice, and tends to keep it in tune. Good articulation in some degree may even be said to take the place of genuine feeling and emotion.

Slovenly articulation, as a rule, means slovenly singing.

Sing your consonants. Make music with them. Get as much sound from them as you can (particularly with L, M, N, R). *This takes time.* It takes time also to articulate clearly consonants which have little or no vocal sound at all, e.g. the explodents P, B, T, D, K, G. A distinct silence should be perceptible *before* these so that the breath may have time to gather and concentrate itself behind the articulation. Then there is a magnificently distinct release. Note also that if this is done properly (with the right intensity), there will be a small escape of breath after each consonant, e.g. 'come' when fully articulated will be sounded almost as 'khum', though the aspirate of course will not amount to a full 'h'.

Remember that consonants, as well as vowels, should be started truly 'in the centre of the note'. Singers who would scorn to a preliminary scoop or slide when beginning a note with a vowel, frequently err when it is a question of a consonant. Words beginning with 'W' also are pitfalls, and especially on high notes, e.g.

woe

(which is compounded of a very close-lip 'oo' and 'oh') might be heard as

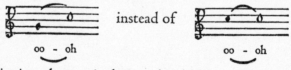

    oo - oh   instead of   oo - oh

In *legato* singing clear articulation should be sought without unnecessarily interrupting the vocal tone. But in certain songs, and especially in passages of narrative or statement, as opposed to passages of sentiment, it is often good to exaggerate verbal definition and separate instead of link the words.

The sibilant 's' must be carefully watched and unanimously articulated. Bennet's Madrigal, 'Thyrsis, sleepest thou?' begins :

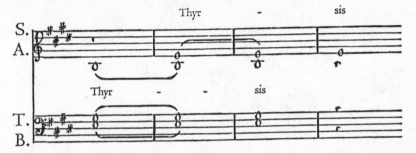

And, unless it is agreed where the final 's' shall occur, each singer taking part will probably finish the word at a different point, prolong the hiss for some time, and the last two bars will be a veritable sea of sibilants. On the other hand, singing is usually deficient in sibilant utterance, as any gramophone choral record will show. Be careful of noun plurals. Often the final voiced 'z' in them can scarcely be distinguished from 's'.

As regards the *timing* of consonants, a valuable rule is that consonants should always be sounded *before* the beat and not on it.

Initial consonants come *before* the note on which their syllable occurs. Likewise final consonants *before* the following note. When a rest is concerned, it as it were cuts off the preceding word, and the final consonant slips in just before it. Applying this to the Bass of the above example, and representing the sustained tone by a horizontal line, and the first beat of each bar by an intersecting vertical line we get :

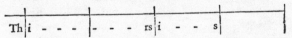

It will thus be seen that the vowel marks the entry of the note, not the consonant. In other words the 'time-spot' of a note is always associated with the vowel. It is most difficult to get a body of singers to be accurate in this matter.

It is essential that the idea should be fully established that the *end* of a verbal note is just as important as the beginning, perhaps more so as far as precision is concerned;* and it requires a very practised technique to ensure that even a single singer, much more a group of singers, shall articulate final consonants at the exact spot that is necessary. It is astonishing, in fact, how difficult a matter this is, and how few singers can be relied upon to do it, or conductors to indicate it. It is quite an art in itself, as a very little experience will show. In instrumental music, of course (or the Italian tongue, which is almost without final consonants), this consideration does not arise, and note-endings are then relatively a simple matter ; but with our language and others it comes to the fore at every turn.

One of our best teachers of speech† suggests an exercise in articulation which can be heartily endorsed. She calls it the 'lipping' exercise, and presents it approximately in these words : 'Imagine you are in a room where some one is asleep and where you may not move or speak aloud for fear of waking the sleeper. There is, however, some one else at the extreme end of the room to whom you must give a message, and give it without any mistake as to meaning. To do so you must summon up all your force of breath, direct it to the very front of the lips, and manage to convey what you wish to say practically by means of mouth shape and movement alone.' What the average singer can scarcely do *with* sound, the really good speaker (or singer) can accomplish *without*. Or nearly so.

Attack and Finish

THE accurate start and ending of a composition or section is one of the most striking features of good *ensemble*.

There should be absolute unanimity in point of entry, and this can only be secured if the singer is *prepared with breath*. He should never start singing while breath is being emitted, or attempt to snatch a breath just before the start. Breath should be taken deliberately and *held* in preparation for attack. At the commencement of a piece a good conductor will make this possible by waiting slightly on the uplifted position of his beat.

---

* And also in regard to continuity and expression—a note should gather and break upon the next note, like a wave, for fine *legato*.

† Miss Marjorie Gullan.

Singers should be able to use both forms of attack:

(1) The clear or ordinary method of attack;

(2) The closed glottis attack.

The glottis attack is occasionally appropriate when a phrase begins with a vowel and a specially *forte*, incisive attack is wanted; but in a general way it should only be used for the purposes of study and not performance. Nothing sounds worse or is more ill placed than to give a glottis attack to every word which happens to start on a vowel. And this is by no means an uncommon habit.

Sometimes phrases must begin with strong, determined accent; sometimes they must appear to glide in.

Sometimes phrases must leave off with almost an effect of accent, i.e. by sustaining the sound loudly, or even *crescendo*, right up to the point of conclusion; sometimes they should drop out almost imperceptibly.

You can neither start nor end well unless you look at the conductor.

Be responsive to the conductor; alert and hearty in carrying out his suggestions. Do not make him feel as if he were trying to move a stone with a straw. You should be as it were on tiptoe; sometimes actually so, ready waiting; or better still, like a bird hovering with outstretched wings, stirring to the slightest breath of wind. Good sight-reading is an essential factor in good choir-singing. Singers who cannot take their eyes off the music are useless in a choir. A good conductor has been said to be one who has the score in his head, not his head in the score. The same applies to the good chorus singer.

A conductor is indispensable for the guiding of ensemble effects, but individual members of a choir should rely largely on their own initiative. Once the normal course of a Madrigal or other composition has been started by the conductor, it should be quite possible, if it remain unvaried, for the singers themselves to continue it without further guidance. They should be able to keep together purely from a sense of time and their ability to take up the various entries. And there should be no difficulty in getting a certain amount of colour as well. This, combined with good voice production, constitutes the requisite efficiency of the individual member, and is the basis upon which the finer choral effects are built. It must be urged that when a conductor is obliged to spend his energy in preserving strict time and indicating every unimportant entry, he does so at the expense of those passages where it is really essential for him to conduct. Moreover, the chances are that he will not even succeed in preserving strict time or getting precise entries. When choristers have no initiative, they are likely to be dull and unresponsive, and if they wait for entries to be indicated before daring to come in, they will be sure to come in as if with profuse apologies, and a half-second or so late. The ideal function of a conductor is to pilot the extraordinary passages of a work where variety is sought and the normal is departed from. Mere mechanical precision should be safely left to the choir. If it cannot be, the choir is so much the less efficient, and its results will be proportionately unsatisfactory.

General Style of singing Madrigals

THE essence of it is *liquidity* of sound; a supple, continuous flow; the perfection of *legato* though it may take a *staccato* form.

Attention has already been drawn to the specially intimate association between the words and music of a Madrigal. Therefore the nearer we can get to the grace and beauty of poetic speech, in Madrigal singing, the better. The bias of expression, in short, should be towards the words rather than the notes. For the music is the garment of the words.

As compared with speech, music has a greater rigidity. Both the length and pitch of notes are fixed. Neither is in speech. So that it is quite fair to say that speech is a more flexible medium than music. But though words must be subject to restraint in song, we should, when singing them, try to retain as much of their freedom as we can; particularly so, in this case, when they are of such primary importance.

Staccato is seldom used in speech, the main attributes of which are undulating, easy movement from word to word, and subtle accentual nuance. So that from the verbal standpoint a Madrigal connects closely with *legato* style. But from the musical standpoint, also, the suitability of *legato* must be stressed. The *melos* of polyphonic music, deriving as it does from plainsong, is perhaps more fitted to the sacred form of the motet than to the Madrigal. It certainly was in the earliest days. By degrees Madrigalian melody developed a more genuinely secular note, and the line of cleavage between sacred and secular became more and more pronounced. But it was never so great as to determine the principle of secularity completely, or fix it firmly in the shape of the Dance, though Ballets were said to be devised 'to be danced to voices'. Consequently, all polyphonic melody has something of plain-song about it, and 'liquid' *legato* utterance being of the very bone and marrow of plain-song, it likewise characterizes not only the expression of a Motet but of a Madrigal. Thus even *staccato* phrasing in a Madrigal must be permeated with a certain *legato* spirit. And *legato*, of course, means far more than the mere sustaining of one note till the next.

Cadences

THE beauty of a Madrigal is often most apparent in its cadences, and particularly in its final cadence. It is here that we have Milton's 'linked sweetness long drawn out'; it is here that the tangled web of sound unravels; that the trend of the music is resolved and its emotion summed up. It is here that the composer presents his chief rhetorical effects, introducing ornament, suspensions and long notes, in contrast to what may have been plain and straightforward before. The cadence is the singer's opportunity. If the audience is to be persuaded, it will most certainly be by the variations of time and tone which are appropriate to the cadence. The effect of a final chord, sung *ppp*, brought on by a *diminuendo* and delayed by a well-proportioned *ritenuto*, is indescribable. But to sing a cadence to perfection the singers must obey the conductor perfectly, and must here, of all places in the composition, watch his suggestions.

Realize, at times, the vanishing point of sound. As in painting, you do not always want hard outlines.

Accent, &c.

ACCENT is the life of music, or rather, is that element in musical interpretation which shows that music has life. Without accent music strikes no chord responsive to our physical nature. It is purely mental, contemplative. Unaccented music only affects us in a mental sense. Some music *is* serene, spiritual, detached. But most music has some connexion with physical emotion, and to rob it of accent is, therefore, in some measure, to rob it of its nature. Accent is as much an element of most music as the notes themselves. We may get an impression of beautiful form, melody, harmony, or even colour from (in its broadest sense) an unaccented performance; but such form is physically lifeless, and may be radically untrue.

When words suggest great energy, great accent must be given to the music. And in the same way music should become less and less accented in proportion as the words suggest less and less animation.

In lively music the *direct* accent should be used.

If I were asked which were the most necessary qualities for a choir to cultivate, I think I should say, in view of their almost invariable absence, that of being able to give direct accent and that of being able to sustain tone evenly. My experience is that nine out of every ten singers do not know what a direct accent is in the sense of $>$ or of the sound having its maximum intensity right at the start. The singer's sense of accent is too often $<>$ or that of a swell, thoroughly desirable when a persuasive or imploring effect is wanted, but quite ill-suited to crisp, lively, or robust passages.

As to the second point, no words can sufficiently impress the importance of sustaining tone evenly. It is a main feature of all good singing and expression worthy of the name. No true expression is possible without it. This is not saying that there must be no variety of tone or accent, but only that all such variety must, in general, be *regularly* achieved and have this sustained, even tone as its basis. Here, again, most singers, particularly basses, realize what they imagine to be sustained tone by a sort of 'pump' or 'swell', which amounts to an underlining of each note, regardless of whether such notes should be underlined or not. This style of singing is so prevalent, especially with church-choir singers, that it might almost be called the 'vocal' style. We plead for a touch of the firmer 'instrumental' style in singing, and for directness where directness is required.*

---

* Even at the risk of confusing the singer it must be said here that, on the other hand, in an absolutely true sense, the 'swell' is the very foundation of good performance, for it represents the principle of growth which applies as much to music as to life.

Notes must not be attacked roughly, but with a sensitive, scarcely-daring *touch*. And they must be instantly open to modification of tone force or any change of expression. This does not

The matter is of such importance that a diagram may be added for further clearness. Take a scale passage:

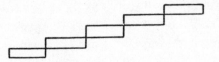

Each section of the above represents a note of the same intensity throughout its length. The breath pressure should not vary on each individual note. At the change of note the vocal cords should be quickly readjusted. There should be no scooping of notes. Perfect *legato* singing is required; but it must not be held to include an *obvious portamento* between notes, such as makes the join of more importance than the notes themselves. *Portamento*, as an effect, is seldom wanted in Madrigal singing, though singers should link notes together far better than they generally do.

Tone which is *not* evenly sustained might be represented as follows:

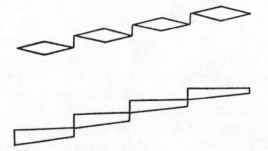

or,

The effect of *crescendos* and *diminuendos* is completely dependent upon this eliminate 'direct' accent. A *sforzando* can quite well be brought under this treatment. Thus, a song and all music may rightly be said to be made up of a series of swells: the swell on the single note, the swell on the phrase, which is the normal form of phrase expression, and the swell on the piece as a whole, the culminating point of which is the 'climax' of the piece. It is only in this way that a 'movement' of sound can be imagined and achieved. But this swell is a very different thing from the 'pumping' referred to above, of which the fault is essentially that it is uncontrolled. Indeed all faults may probably be summed up in this single word.

It is a very good habit to 'feed' a sustained note with tone on each beat so that it is something like

$$\frac{1 \quad 2 \quad 3 \quad 4}{> <> <> <> <}$$

though of course it must be scarcely apparent. This serves the double purpose of pulsing the music more intensely, and also of preventing the sound from becoming enfeebled at the end, which generally happens in poor singing, with consequent inability to make final consonants clear.

perfectly-controlled tone. For, in a *crescendo*, if the breath pressure is re-laxed ever so little, the effect is immediately destroyed; the unity of the *crescendo* is lost. In going, say, from *p* to *f* by way of *crescendo*, though the *f* may be arrived at at the proper time, it does not follow that an effect of *crescendo* has been secured. It is the sense of continuous, *regular* growth of sound that is wanted; not a series of spasmodic efforts. Similarly, in a *diminuendo*, the effect to be aimed at is a *regular* decrease of sound, which is as dependent on sustained tone as a *crescendo*. *Sustained tone is a question of breath control.* A diagram of a good *legato crescendo* and *diminuendo* might be given as the following:

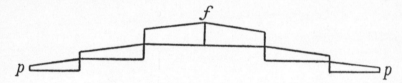

and for a *staccato crescendo* and *diminuendo*:

in which the black portions indicate the momentary cessation of the sound. Thus, fundamentally, *staccato* means *legato*; and *legato* means *staccato*.

To which may be added von Bülow's excellent saying, '*Crescendo* means piano; *diminuendo* means *forte*.'

Pianissimo passages frequently give the impression of going to pieces, and this is merely due to losing sight of the line of tone from its being irregular, wavering, or even broken.

It is infinitely harder to sing a phrase with equal and even tone through-out, than to vary it. There is something very beautiful in a flow of sound which is so musical that the words pass almost unheeded; so smooth as to be almost pointless; so calm (even in the grandest sonorities) as to appear that the singer was singing without knowing it and was even listening to himself. Singing of such a character is not often wanted outside sacred music; but the singer will do well to have command over it.

If you vary your tone, do so with a purpose.

As a rule nuances should be made gradually and with fine sense of proportion.

Violent and sudden effects of contrast are hardly ever appropriate.

A single note unduly standing out may destroy the whole unity of the phrasing.

The two main principles of musical accent are based as follows: (1) that higher notes require greater effort to produce than lower notes, and therefore should be accented in preference to lower notes; (2) that longer notes are more important than shorter notes, and should therefore be accented in preference to shorter notes; or briefly, the highest and longest notes should be accented.

As a rule the principal accent of a phrase coincides with both the highest and longest notes.

The above does not apply to the last note of a phrase where there is varied treatment as regards accent. Length of note is no factor here.

Never rush on to an accent, nor hurry the first note of a phrase if it begins on an upbeat. Take time for it to 'gather', after the manner of the 'initial' notes of medieval hymn-tunes, which were usually prolonged, relative to the other notes.

Accented notes must be taken deliberately and sometimes even retarded a little to produce their greatest effect. Otherwise good performance is often marred by hurrying the ends of phrases or rushing on to accented notes. The result of this is to introduce an element of trivial agitation into the performance, which is seldom called for by the nature of the music itself. Such effects must always lack *breadth*; and breadth is characteristic of most, perhaps all, fine music. Fine music may be agitated, but it will scarcely be for a single note or two. In all probability it will be throughout a whole passage; so that the variations of time which will express this agitation should be distributed throughout the passage. Variations of time (*accelerando* and *ritenuto*) as a rule should be so proportioned between the notes affected that though the variation is felt it should be impossible to perceive at what precise point the variation takes place.

Take care of short notes; long notes will look after themselves. Most people have a tendency to hurry the shorter notes of a phrase. Short notes (quavers as compared to minims, crotchets, &c.) should be given their full proportionate value, even lengthened a little, particularly in expressive passages. In the following example, for instance, at the words 'When death approached', the quavers are very liable to be hurried. If they are, the solemnity of the passage is completely lost.

The Silver Swan—ORLANDO GIBBONS

A fine performance is distinguished more, perhaps, by a fine sense of time, than anything else.

Even time, which is only the portal of rhythm, is not a thing that you *count*, but a thing that you *feel*. It is decided by a *feeling* for proportion. And it is the same with *all* the elements of music. A singer's *looks* show how he is performing the music. If he appear limp and listless, for instance, you may know that it is physically impossible for him to give determined accents or strong rhythm. Herbert Spencer has very clearly shown in his essay, 'The Origin and Function of Music', that the origin of song is emotion—that song in fact is the language of emotion. Behind all song—all song that touches—is emotion. Singers who cannot enter into the feeling of their song can never express the essential part of it.

Singers should be careful not to breathe at the expense of the time, when it is required to take breath, and *no rest is indicated where it may be done*. It is a common fault under these circumstances to give full value to the note preceding the breath, so that no time is left to breathe; but breath has to be taken, and in consequence the strict pulse of the movement suffers. It may be only to an infinitesimal degree, but it is sufficient to break the rhythmic flow. This fault is most noticeable in Ballets and compositions where the rhythm of the parts is coincident and the regular metrical element pronounced. To illustrate the point by an example: the first section of Morley's 'My Bonny Lass' ends at the double-bar, and is noted as follows:

It is necessary to continue with the repetition of the section, *pp*, without delay; but it will be found that the majority of singers, if not cautioned, will give the semibreve its full value, and so are quite unprepared to start the next phrase at the proper time.* What they should do is to deliberately sing the semibreve bar as though it were

When a rest is given after a note it may generally be taken that the note should have its full value. When no rest is given, but the point is evidently the end of a phrase, the note should be shortened to allow for breathing.

Be as careful of rests as of notes. 'There is no music in a rest, that I know of,' said Ruskin, 'but there is the making of music in it.' A rest is not only an occasion for breath recovery. It can nearly always be taken as a *sign* for a vital entry, or insistence upon the phrase which follows it. And it is sometimes used by the Madrigalists as a distinct point of expression before or after the word 'sigh', as in Wilbye's 'When Chloris heard'. The French, indeed, call a rest 'un soupir'.

---

* To the average choir-singer the last note of a phrase, or particularly of a section, often yields delightful opportunity of *tenuto* and *crescendo*. He seems to feel that he is allowed to sing this note as heartily as he pleases, and to hold on to it as long as he likes.

Verbal Phrasing

THE drift of a poem as a whole is often obscured by musical setting. To learn precisely what he is singing about the singer should therefore consider the words apart from the music, and express their meaning first of all in speech. A preliminary to the performance of any song should be the perfect speaking of the poetry, or as near to this as one can get.

It is an interesting experiment to speak a phrase—any ordinary bit of conversation will do; then, if it be written down, to read it aloud. Provided it was really 'meant', the spoken phrase will 'carry along' exactly as the stream of thought dictates. The words will follow each other in (if it could be analysed) an amazing variety of *nuance* and accent; and we shall accept them as true verbal expression, about which, as with all true things, there is really nothing to be said.

But if the speaker reads his own words, we may have a good deal to say about it. It will probably lack movement; be stiff and monotonous, and appear *untrue*. Almost certainly it will not be the exact equivalent of the phrase that was imagined in the first place.

Take the matter a step further and sing the phrase, and it will become even more artificial than when it was read, having but slight resemblance to the original.

There is, of course, very great difficulty in reproducing even one's own thought, when the precise experience that called it forth is no longer the stimulus. But this the artist should be able to do, and is required to do with other people's thought as well as his own.

Though music is a language of sound, having undoubtedly its own sense and logic, it is hard for the average person to apply the test of truth to it, mainly through sheer lack of familiarity and use. But we use words all day long, and any one can ask himself when he recites or sings, 'Are these words natural—should I speak like that?' and be his own critic with at any rate a fair measure of success.

It is not suggested here that poetry and commonplace conversation are the same. Poetry has longer sweeps of phrase; more inflamed emotion. It reflects rarer moments, weightier situations, and so employs a certain dignity of expression foreign to ordinary speech. But poetry does not cut adrift from nature. It depends upon the same principles of rhythm and balance and accent as does speech. It only states them in a higher form.

Let the Madrigal singer, then, continuously question the naturalness of his words. And if they pass the test, considerably more than half the battle of fine performance will have been won.

Musical Phrasing*

REMEMBER that (in some degree) a *crescendo* should generally be made when a phrase rises; and a *diminuendo* should be made when a phrase falls. This is the most elementary rule of expression, and the most far-reaching.

Bear in mind the unity of the phrase.

Notes never stand apart by themselves. They are always related to other notes. A phrase is a series of related notes.

When notes, in their delivery, are made to appear disjointed or disconnected by failure to observe true expression, i.e. the rise and fall of a phrase, *legato*, accent, &c., the phrase loses its unity and meaning. It is, in short, non-existent. Ill-adjusted accents, however, can easily destroy the phrase-unit.

On the other hand, phrases should be clear cut. Complete phrases should never be connected with one another; sub-phrases hardly ever. Mere breath-taking, even if it occur at the junction of phrases, is not sufficient here. It is quite possible to breathe at the proper place, and yet give the impression of connecting phrases which should be distinct. But it should also be said that breath may be taken during a phrase in such a way that the continuity of the phrase remains undisturbed.

Most singers have a tendency to run the shorter sub-phrases into one another, e.g. the following Tenor phrase from Munday's Madrigal, 'Lightly she whipped':

Did en - ter - tain their sweet har-mo-ny, . . did en - ter - tain . . . .

* Singers and indeed all musicians are advised to read Mathis Lussy's *Musical Expression* (Messrs. Novello & Co.), an extraordinarily stimulating book, one of the best on the subject, though written many years ago.

In this the first phrase evidently ends at the comma (bar 3). Here the singers would, in all probability, take breath of themselves; but, unless corrected, they would also probably make a *crescendo* on the long B♭; for singers almost invariably feel that they are entitled to let their voices 'go' on a long note. The result of this would be that these phrases would appear connected, whereas if the proper expression were made (as indicated above), the phrases would be clearly distinguished. In passing, it may seem that the composer has given too long a note and stress to the light final syllable of the word harmony. But if the phrase be considered as

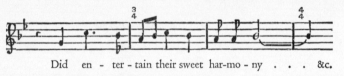

Did   en - ter - tain their sweet har-mo - ny . . . &c.

there is no difficulty in accepting it.

Take another instance from the same Madrigal, the Bass phrase from the refrain :

Long   live   fair   O-ri - a - - na, long live   fair   O - ri -

Here the first phrase ends at the word 'Oriana' on the low G; but the singers, on account of the short time given them for breathing, will probably get carried along to the second phrase, forgo a breath and slur the syllables 'na⌢long'.

In some cases, between phrases, where there is not time to breathe, the vocal tone should be momentarily stopped in order to make clear that the phrases are distinct.

From the foregoing it may be gathered that it is generally necessary to taper the ends of sub-phrases by means of a *diminuendo*; and, also, between phrases to make a distinct break in the sound, usually by a breath. The tapering of the ends of phrases is a most important point, for on it depends very considerably the evidence of interplay between the phrases. The entry of one phrase, in imitative passages, often occurs near the end of another phrase, and the entry is obscured if there is no lightening of the ends of

phrases ; while the contrary, of course, holds good, that entries are rendered more apparent if the other parts give way in a natural manner. The
chief thing in polyphonic music, as far as the listener is concerned, is a
clear definition of the extremes of phrase. The strongest point of phrases,
however, is usually towards the middle.

Munday's Madrigal furnishes us again with the following close imitative passage—a good example of the overlapping of short phrases :

We have put expression marks to the above that it may be seen how the
voices should give way, and, in so doing, enable each other to come to the
fore and appear in turn as the chief feature of the web of sound.

The interplay, then, of the different voices of a Madrigal is chiefly

shown by observing the principal accents and the rise and fall of tone of
the phrase. These accents are, to the ear, what some visible sign would be
to the eye. They point out the phrases. If phrases are sung with the same
amount of tone throughout, it is hard to avoid the impression that the
composition is formed of 'lumps' of harmony, whereas the impression to
be conveyed is that it is formed of 'layers' of melody. This is the all-
important point in Madrigal singing, and almost the whole of Madrigal
expression is subservient to it.

    To insist still further. In the following passage from Ellis Gibbons's
'Oriana' Madrigal:

Long live fair Oriana—ELLIS GIBBONS. No. 4 of 'The Triumphs of Oriana', 1601

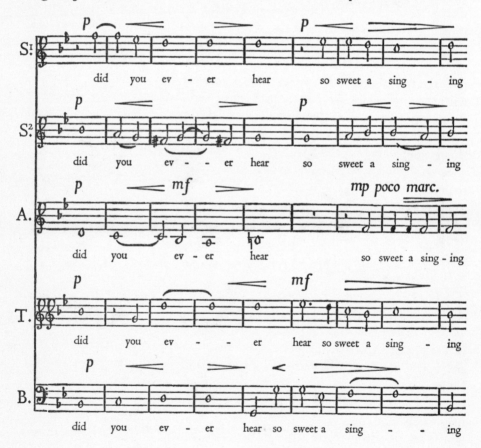

we see all the voices apparently coming to a close on the chord of G major in the fifth bar. But only apparently. In reality the Tenor part is in the course of its phrase at this point, and instead of making a *diminuendo* in common with the other voices it must work against them with a distinct *crescendo* towards the climax of the phrase (E♭).

In the notation of old music and particularly of old religious music the rhythmic periods are scarcely as evident as in modern music with its more striking rhythmic effects. There is often a monotonous treatment of note-value: minims or crotchets, or whatever it may be, succeeding each other without much variety. It may therefore be difficult to realize that such notes are grouped in phrases. But they are certainly so grouped, and it is disregard of the fact that often makes the performance of polyphonic music so insufferably dull. If the singer puts no life into the phrase—and this is what it amounts to—how shall the listener be impressed with any sense of vitality in the music? The singer, however, has a great advantage over the instrumental performer in that the verbal phrase usually coincides with the musical phrase, so that intelligent verbal delivery at the same time defines the extremes of the musical phrase. To phrase well, much more, of course, is required than to define the extremes of phrase; but, at any rate, this is something on the way.

Keep the music moving. Feel that it is in splendid movement from start to finish.

Slow up, if you will; never slow down. There is a difference.

Relation of Words to Notes

IT has been shown how free madrigalian melody is, and how, with infi-nitely varied rhythmic groupings, the composer adjusts the music to the words, so that the musical phrase is generally a perfect counterpart of the verbal phrase. And since polyphony is based upon concord, there are seldom any harmonic reasons for disturbing or modifying the melodic accent; for concord can adapt itself to almost any accent, whereas appoggiaturi or unprepared dissonances involve distinct accents of their own which may easily run counter to those of the words. Thus from all aspects the words are free to preserve their own individuality, and polyphonic music clearly stands as the best that has so far been devised for vocal purposes, if by that we mean a music whose special function it is to combine with words. We have therefore to do little else than apply the rhythmic urge of the verbal phrase to the musical phrase regardless of harmony or even of position or length of note in the melody.

In practice we find that the verbal phrase ebbs and flows from accent to accent in the shape of main pivot words, or such words as we stress to bring out the particular meaning that we wish. Thus, as a preliminary to singing (to further insist upon the method), we cannot do better than read aloud the words of the lyric several times, till we are quite at one with their sense, and the natural flow and accent has been caught.

Let us take the short lyric of Wilbye's Madrigal, 'Adieu, sweet Amarillis', and italicize the chief words :

> *Adieu*, sweet Amarillis !
> For since to *part* your will is,
> O heavy, *heavy* tiding !
> *Here* is for me no biding.
> Yet *once* again, ere that I part with you,
> *Adieu*, sweet Amarillis ; sweet, adieu !

Allowing them to dominate the musical expression, we should get, if we took the Soprano part, something like this :

Adieu, sweet Amarillis—WILBYE

It is not always so easy a matter to determine the expression. Still, a good solution is generally possible on these lines, remembering that one *main* accent should dominate a phrase, though sub-accents can and do occur;*

* These are not noted in the example so that a confusion of signs may be avoided.

remembering also that the end of a *diminuendo* should not tail off weakly, but be as firm in its own way as the stronger part of the phrase, and that these rises and falls, which may often be fittingly accompanied by a little urging and slackening of pace, should not take an exaggerated form.

Even in light music this same sort of phrase-building happens. Thus in:

Pleasure is a wanton thing—BATESON

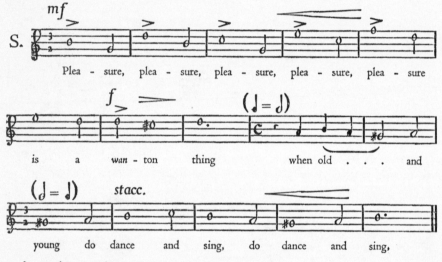

we have the words,

> Pleasure is a *wanton* thing
> When old and young do dance and sing,

where the chief accent of the complete phrase might be held to occur upon the word 'wanton'. Hence the rhythmic scheme would be as above.

Or we should have in this Ballet:

My Bonny Lass—MORLEY

This treatment, of course, besides being true to the verbal structure, has the further very important function of binding the notes together and giving them continuity.

On the other hand, phrases, particularly in triples, are sometimes so short, that it suffices to do little more than give a pronounced metrical accent to the first of the bar or group, as in this passage :

On the plains, fairy trains—WEELKES

now   they dance,   *now*   they prance,   *now*   they dance,   *now*   they prance

Here phrase-building in the larger sense has scarcely to be considered. Indeed, the lilt of the passage depends upon full advantage being taken of the strong and weak syllables of the separate words. It is only when a certain *sostenuto* or dignity of expression has to be maintained that accents have to be led up to or left in a gradual way. Then weak syllables may have to be strengthened so that they become as strong as their stronger brethren.

To be quite clear about this, though at some risk of repetition, let us take these phrases from Weelkes's 'Methinks I hear':

dis - till - ing sil - v'ring sound, dis - till - ing   sil - v'ring sound,

Here each phrase must be kept intact by a swell, having its centre about the middle of the phrase, disregarding what may happen to the weak syllables. Or, in a further passage from the same madrigal, the growing eloquence of :

And . . with   soul - pleas - ing   Mu - - sic

forbids any weakening on the unimportant word 'with' or the second
syllable of 'pleasing'. And it is not only that the music demands it; the
right delivery of the words demands it also. No orator would allow his
voice to drop in such a situation. Otherwise he would get a mere niggling
subservience to individual words and lose the spirit of the phrase.

Nevertheless, in Madrigal singing, it must be allowed that it is very
difficult to get anything like fixed principles of accentuation, which would
give us fixed practice in interpretation; and it is of course the combination of verbal and musical expression which creates or at least enhances
the difficulty. When one thinks that one is on the road to a perfectly
sure grasp of the subject—such as would enable one to say at all times:
this or that note should be accented, this or that note should be passed
over as unimportant—one is confronted by a passage concerning which
one has woefully to admit that 'circumstances alter cases'. It would be
a very satisfactory thing—and one is always striving towards it—to be
able to attain to a perfectly 'fool-proof' science of expression. But
while being able to say a good deal that seems valid and may help, one
knows that it never covers the whole ground, and perhaps cannot.

For instance, in speaking of the expression of dissonance in an earlier
section, it was suggested that the point of dissonance is the point of accent,
and there is little doubt but that this holds, musically, in nine cases out of
ten. Yet what are we to do in the case of these three variants of practically
the same music, which occur in Morley's four-part Madrigal, 'Ho, who
comes here'. They represent conventional cadential treatment. Here it is
in one form, not the most usual, inasmuch as the dissonant note is a
repeated note and not tied :

In this it is evident that it is quite right to accent the G of the lower Soprano on the word 'coming'. A little further on we get the same sort of dissonance in the form more generally met with, that is to say, as a suspension tied on to its resolution :

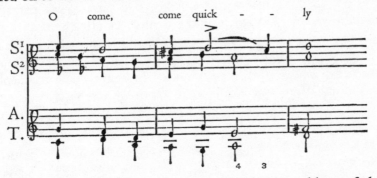

Here there seems nothing for it but to accent the second beat of the bar, which is not in accordance with our typical dissonantal expression:

Then later we have :

where the whole apple-cart seems upset by musically false accent in which the resolution of the dissonance must receive the accent and the long dissonant note is given to the unimportant word 'and'.

No consistent treatment seems possible here, as regards dissonance; and we must simply take refuge in the advice 'Sing as you would speak'—accent the words naturally—never mind the music. Indeed such instances seem to show that the Madrigalist paid little attention to musical expression as such, however we may regard it now; and that his only concern was with the accent of the words. So that not only with rhythm, but with harmony, the safest course and perhaps that most in accordance with the intention of the composer is to focus attention on the words and let the music, as regards accent, take care of itself. This is a little chastening to the musician who has been taught to think that music is a finer form of expression than words and should rule the roast, but still he must accept the supremacy of the words.

Again, there seems to be no doubt but that, musically speaking, though pitch is not a greatly determining feature of accent, relative length of note is. When a series of short notes is arrested by a longer note, that note becomes specially significant and so has a tendency to bear a dynamic accent as well, which may be indulged in if no violence is done to the verbal phrasing. Thus, in Wilbye's 'Sweet Honey-sucking Bees', the little phrase

O   be - ware   of that!

can well be accented on the dotted crotchet and also, in a lesser degree, on the final minim.* But it should be remarked that the last note of a phrase, which is often the longest, frequently has no claim to an accent. By no manner of means could an accent be given to the final note here:

Draw on, sweet night—WILBYE

I   con - se - crate . .   it   whol - ly,

---

* This also offers a convenient text for considering another point with relation to accents, viz. their *balance* in a phrase. Though both the B♭ and the G should be accented, they must not be *equally* accented, for this would destroy the unity of the phrase. In other words, there is room for only one chief accent in a phrase; other accents take subsidiary places. Thus phrases are built up towards an objective, which often, though by no means always, occurs about the middle of the phrase, as in the above example. It would, of course, be possible to maintain that, in this particular phrase, the word 'that' and not the word 'beware' should have the chief stress. In that case the B♭ would bear a lesser accent than the G. No phrase can serve two accentual masters.

We may admit, then, the generally superior importance of long notes, but we have often to acknowledge that a short note has the chief claim to emphasis.

In the opening strain of Dowland's 'Awake, sweet love', the fervour of the word 'Awake' is obviously the dominating feature, and the accentuation is best upon these lines :

though it means stressing one of the shorter notes of the phrase. This would never have suggested itself as a purely musical treatment, which would have selected rather the first and highest F as the chief note of the bar; and it shows how the verbal modifies the musical phrasing.

This phrase is another instance of the difficulty that every Madrigal singer will have, at times, of abandoning the musical accent in favour of the verbal. Noted as it is, it would never occur to any one to accent the second minim of the bar. But if we bar the phrase as follows :

it assumes quite another complexion, and we are easily prepared for this special accenting.*

* There is nothing wrong with bars if they are merely accepted as a sign of accent to the note immediately following. Indeed, it is a convenient way of indicating it, apart from the further use that bars have of showing the reader or performer what is being done by every one at a particular moment. But though accent is implied in modern barring, another principle, which is distinctly cramping and bad, has crept in, viz. that of accentual regularity. This can perhaps be accounted for, historically, by the fact that bars began to be systematically used at a time when dance rhythms also began to be used by serious composers. And as these rhythms were a predominant feature of the 'new music' of the seventeenth century, it became fixed in men's minds that the bar *meant* metrical regularity; and this use of the bar has entirely swamped its other use, that of merely indicating accent, and as well—and this is the most important consideration—it absolutely killed rhythmic freedom itself. But a veritable renaissance of rhythm is in progress, and, before long, it seems likely that Elizabethan methods will be completely re-established, and each part will once again be free to move according to the law of its individual being.

The singer must learn to appreciate what is, in reality, a possible ambiguity of meaning in many phrases, which must often be regarded as a sort of neutral ground for the words to impress *their* individuality upon. Words vary their meaning according to stress. It is the same with note-patterns. And it is best to have no fore-imagined ideas of the musical expression, as we saw in 'Awake, sweet love'. The musician must always be subordinate to the poet.

If we take this phrase of Byrd :

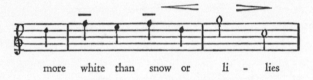

more   white   than   snow   or   li - lies

we see that the crotchets are quite capable of being accented in other group forms, thus :

wed - ded   to   will   is   wit - less,

or

Da - mon,   Chlo - e's   sweet   shep - herd,

though the phrase as a whole takes the same shape with the note G as the objective.

Byrd also writes his phrase thus (of course without bars) :

more   white   than   snow   or   li - lies

but this would not alter the accentuation, or bring an accent on the long final note. The nature of this last note is almost bound to be feminine and unaccented, as will be seen if we write it in its natural barring :

more   white   than   snow   or   li - lies,   . . .

where the final note is perceived to be prolonged merely for harmonic purposes.

These latter examples exemplify the musical accent which is appropriate to a long note after a series of short ones, and the long note is also rein-forced by being the highest note as well. There is, of course, nothing par-ticularly important about the word 'lilies'. The most important word is perhaps 'white'. But in this case the musical expression may well dominate the phrasing, as the natural verbal accents are sufficiently preserved.

A more difficult phrase to express is that given by Byrd at another appearance of the same words:

more white than snow   or . .   li   -   -   -   -   -   lies.

Here if we attempt to apply the principle of stressing relatively long notes we should get a false verbal accent on 'or', and the best way to regard the phrase is probably:

more white than snow   or   li   -   -   -   -   -   lies,

in which the phrase as a whole is unified by a general rise and fall, though this must not be extravagantly carried out.

This last example introduces another principle, just as vital in its way, though contradictory to that of emphasizing long notes. It is this. Just as a long note is emphatic by reason of position, so also may a group of short notes be, drawing attention to themselves, as it were, by sudden 'intrusion'. If we wish to 'explain' our expression in the foregoing example, we can do so on these lines—the long note being looked upon as preparation for emphasis on the following quaver group.

A very frequent *cliché* in Madrigalian melody is:

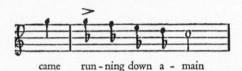

came run - ning down a - main

It occurs times without number, and must nearly always be accented as above, in accordance with the need of ticking off, or delineating a group of relatively short notes.

An interesting little phrase, which, in a nutshell, may serve to put the singer on his guard, is the following:

and sud - den - ly,

where, by reason of length and bar position, the last note seems as if it could do no other than bear the chief accent. But if we view it without prejudice, and rearrange the phrase thus, we see that it really stands for:

As regards the notes it is quite possible, of course, as with the ambiguous phrase on p. 72, to treat them with the accent on the final C. If they were fitted to words as follows:

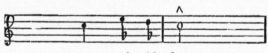

crown - ed with flowers,

they would have to be so accented. Neither of the two forms is unmusical.

If will be found, indeed, that, though we cannot reduce it to a perfectly
simple system, most of the musical expression required by the words, in
Madrigals, *can* be justified on purely musical grounds, provided we are
not hide bound, or tied up with rigid barring. We are always unwise to
take things at their face value, and imagine that 'barbarities' of setting
exist, before we are perfectly sure that they are implied. If, however, there
seems to be no way of justifying the music given to the words, the onus
is on the composer, not on us. It was his business to accentuate the music
aright. He usually does. It is ours to accentuate the words.

It is very hard, doubtless, at first glance, to see the right musical accentuation of the Alto part in such a passage as this (which must be one of
our final examples), where we get the very extreme of polyphonic practice,
with, in the second and third bars, the verbal and musical accents apparently
at absolutely cross purpose:

Die now, my heart—MORLEY

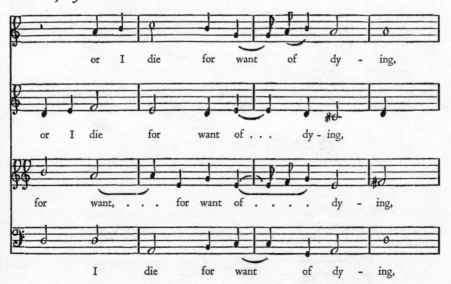

But this barring does not truly cover the Alto part (or indeed the others), and perhaps we can only realize how completely independent it is, if we see it, put into the passage, barred in its proper form:

A conductor is almost useless under such circumstances. The integrity of the expression must simply be left to the singers. But the composer is right enough, and we should be wrong if we look upon his point of view as absurd. And if we are asked by the Madrigalist to deal with such a phrase as:

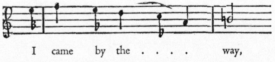

are we to think that our compliance is being rather too much imposed upon, or that it would perhaps have been better to note the phrase as:

We have to adapt ourselves to the situation that confronts us. That is the long and short of it. And in nearly every case a good job can be made of it if we try. The 'music and sweet poetry' do agree.

But, if perchance our musical nature is so hyper-sensitive that we really cannot allow the words to impose what we *think* is a false accent upon the music, we can always take refuge in giving no accent at all.* It is a negative policy, but it would still leave the main part of the words and music intact. As we have said elsewhere, the glow of life comes through accent and shading. Yet a quite impressive performance can be given without such things; as on the organ, where only the length and pitch of note are defined and dynamic expression need not enter at all. But it is no small matter to realize well even these purely formal elements in music. It is indeed a very big matter, involving that most difficult of accomplishments, a steady and effective stream of sound, which, in the case of singing, is generally not to be compared to what the organ gives us. After all, nine-tenths of 'expression' simply consists in making the notes clear. The rest is an adornment, the personal reaction of the interpreter to the music, rather than the music itself. The only fixed, abiding, absolute thing in music is that which can be absolutely noted on paper: its shape and design —in other words its idea, and this is independent of the variabilities and vagaries of expression.

In the face of such a statement, the performer may feel that his stature is sadly diminished beside that of the poet or composer. Are his little points and accents, then, not worth while? We must give him heart again by quoting Byrd's counsel to those to whom he commended his *Psalmes, Songs and Sonets* of 1611: 'Only this I desire,' he said, 'that you will be as careful to hear them well expressed, as I have been both in the composing and correcting of them. Otherwise the best song that ever was made will seem harsh and unpleasant; for that the well expressing of them either by voices or instruments is the life of our labours, which is seldom or never well performed at the first singing or playing.' So that we may proceed, refreshed by this friendly encouragement from the great composer.

* Some languages in fact require little or no accent, notably the Latin languages, which are vitalized by inflexion rather than by accent. English, of course, is an accented language; but it is worth noting that polyphony is by nature allied to religion, rather than to secular expression, and that Latin, the language of the Church, had by far the most influence upon it, formally. The trend and spirit of polyphony, therefore, may be said to be non-accentual, rather than accentual.

Melismatic Melody

THE relation of words to notes may further be considered under the above heading.

The practice of the Madrigalists is very varied in regard to the decorative aspect of melody, and it ranges from a simple note for syllable treatment, as in:

through such a type as this, which seeks to give realistic expression to a word:

Sweet Suffolk Owl—VAUTOR

to genuinely melismatic or florid melody, which has little or no connexion with pictorial effect, but is used solely for the purposes of musical rhetoric, such as:

Love would discharge—BYRD

with its masculine (◡ —) ending, or

Wedded to will—BYRD

and not by rea - - - - - - son

when the ending is feminine (– ◡).

Such examples as the two latter undoubtedly have their genesis in Plainsong tradition; and they occur mostly in the works of Byrd, who, in his choral writing, represented an earlier style than those of the Madrigalists in general, though, in instrumental music, he was so great an innovator.

The Madrigalists, indeed, held this particular kind of melody up to ridicule, if we may take Morley's comment upon it as a prevalent view, for he says, in giving rules for 'dittying', 'We must also have a care to applie the notes to the words, as in singing there be no barbarisme committed, that is that we cause no syllable which is by nature short, be expressed by manie notes or one long note, nor no long syllable bee expressed with a short note:* but in this fault do the practitioners erre more grossly, then in any other, for you shal find few songs wherein the penult syllables of these words *Dominus, Angelus, filius, miraculum, gloria,* and such like are not expressed with a long note, yea manie times with a whole dossen of notes, and though one should speak of fortie he shud not say much amisse: which is a grosse barbarisme, and yet might be easily amended.' What Morley condemns is exactly and almost invariably what the Plain-song melodist with his far purer sense of vocal style would have done. The truth is that a number of notes given to a word or syllable does not make that particular word accented above a word or syllable which is only set to one note. It is a matter of accentuation and not of form, as the Plain-song writer knew full well. It may even be said that, in one sense, the delaying of the accented word or syllable, as in the first Byrd example, tends to give it additional weight. At any rate it is certain that we soon get accustomed to this melodic treatment and enjoy its unfettered, stimulating quality. The humblest article or preposition may thus be honoured with a decorative flourish, which would be reserved by moderns for only the mightier

---

* Fortunately, Morley often fails to abide by his own precept.

members of the verbal community. The extreme of this treatment may be seen in this example:

In crystal towers—BYRD

it   pleas-eth her   to . . . .   stay

where the quite unimportant preposition 'to' is raised to a high degree of musical dignity in the vocal phrase, producing a certain compensation and balance between the words and notes, and giving maximum strength to the phrase as a whole.

There is a vast difference, of course, between this sort of florid handling, which throughout represents what may be called essential melody, and the mere surface adornment, in the shape of arpeggio or scale passage, of certain types of post-Madrigalian melody. It is always vocal and not instrumental, and never descends to the 'pitiful, thin' meanderings of conventional coloratura or variations.

These melismata occur generally, as Morley noted, on the penultimate, or antepenultimate syllables of the main cadences, or they may be reserved for the conclusion of the song, just as a column receives its chief decoration upon its topmost member, the capital. The good wine is kept to the last, so that the final touch of embellishment may come with the greatest effect. As we have already indicated, they must not be confused with word-painting, which may occur anywhere and is usually taken advantage of when the occasion presents itself. Such word-painting is nearly always concerned with some idea of physical animation and generally starts upon a metrically strong beat which should be emphasized, thus:

Hope of my heart—WARD

still   thun - - - der forth

But the smooth undulation of a melisma generally starts upon a weak beat, and should be expressed by a swell.

Help, Lord, for wasted are those men—BYRD

When smooth-est he doth . . . . smile

The foregoing example is chosen for illustration because it, as well, exhibits a feature that may need elucidating. In bar 4 we find a repeated note which has to be sung without any fresh verbal articulation. This presents a difficulty which is sometimes evaded by simply tying the two notes, as:

or completely separating them, as:

Neither of these methods is adequate. The characteristic *legato* of the melody must be preserved while the repetition is made quite distinct; and this can be done by putting a little extra pressure on the second note, together with perhaps the slightest touch of aspirate. All of which can be achieved without any discontinuity in the tone.

From our remarks as to accent and emphasis it will be seen once more that the Madrigal singer must be prepared to stress words at any place in the bar regardless of pitch or even length of note. The most important word may go to the shortest note, or what seems to be the least important word to a whole group of notes.

Thus, according to generally conceived notions something like topsy-turvydom in verbal setting exists between the practice of the Madrigalists and the moderns, and it is sometimes hard to resist the feeling that, though polyphony is said to be based on words, it often seems utterly to distort them. Yet in reality all the singer has to do is to accept the principle that polyphony *is* based on words, and not words on polyphony. And if he will frankly allow the verbal accent to dominate, abandoning a purely musical outlook—or perhaps we should say a 'conventionally' musical outlook, based merely on dance rhythms—he will soon see that he is scarcely ever distressed with the result; but that, on the contrary, a variety and interest, and a rightness, will emerge that is little short of a revelation to many. But it needs very wary, careful practice to become so master of the notes that they are entirely obedient to verbal exigency; and it is almost impossible to get the expression necessary for the finest performance simply from choir work. That is why one seldom or never hears an adequate choral performance of a Madrigal, where the words suffer no travesty but appeal in their full poetic loveliness. It is perhaps a little tedious to study Madrigalian phrasing apart from the ensemble. But in the solo Ayres of the period, particularly in those of Dowland, the singer can find most attractive material upon which to develop a true style. If he supplement his choral practice by this, and, still better, by an acquaintance with Plainsong as well, he will not only see the true drift of Madrigal singing far better than he otherwise would, but will gain results that are very much in advance of the average.

Syllabic Distribution

WHEN several notes go to a syllable, the way in which these notes are distributed is often a source of difficulty to the singer. For example:

Since Robin Hood—WEELKES

Carol—BYRD

This method of arranging notes to syllables is so different from the modern method that singers (and even editors of old music) are apt to think that there has been some mistake, and so they alter the distribution to suit the modern way. Unless singers are warned, they might be likely to sing the foregoing phrases as:

The essential difference between the old method (as shown in the first group of examples) and the modern method (as shown in the second group) is that in the former the syllable starts from an *un*accented beat, whereas in modern music the syllable always starts from an accented beat. The effect of this is to make these unaccented beats much more prominent than they would be in modern vocal music, *even to the extent of displacing the normal accents of the bar*. The old method, by its irregularity of accent, conduces to vigour of movement; the modern method, by its regularity, gains flow, but assuredly at the expense of strength.

These Elizabethan 'underlayings' of the words, as they are called, should be interpreted by an accent on the first note. If they occur in a pointed, rhythmic passage, such as in the Weelkes, the accent should be quite marked; but if the sense of the passage is more sweeping, as in the Byrd, less accent should be given.

The question of breath-taking also enters into this matter. There is no difficulty in breath-taking in a Madrigal, because the *caesura* (or comma) always comes before a comparatively weak beat or part of the beat. But with the modern method there is often no time to breathe owing to an unnatural *caesura*. Thus, in a sacred song of Bach, in accordance with the composer's own practice, though we quote here from an edition with English words, the tenor is asked to sing:

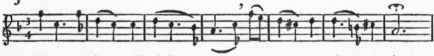

Up, up! my heart! with glad - - ness Sing what was done to - day.

In this it is evident that, if breath has to be taken after 'gladness', the rhythm must suffer. There is simply no time for it, and this applies to numberless modern instances. The Elizabethans would have written:

glad - ness Sing . . what

which creates no difficulty.

This small matter of breath-taking shows perhaps more than anything how post-Madrigalian composers fell away from vocal tradition and adopted instead an instrumental outlook. Indeed, it was admitted in so many words by Beethoven, who said that he always heard his ideas on an instrument, never on the voice.

It is a nice point whether the moderns have not only weakened vocal music, structurally, by placing notes to syllables in the way that they do, but have adopted a method which is radically false. If we are decided that an unaccented beat is naturally connected with an accented beat, and not vice versa—that in this sequence of notes, for example,

the natural connexion between them is as shown by the slurs, then it seems to follow that syllables should commence on the unaccented beats (as the polyphonic composers made them) when there is a question of distributing unaccented notes in this way. The fusion between words and music is more natural, and, consequently, the result more perfect when this is done. The reason for altering the practice of the older musicians was probably to get unanimous accent in all the parts (because the mere fact of beginning a syllable on any note tends to make that note accented). But the older musicians did not want unanimous accent. 'The separate voice parts ... were purposely put together in such a way as to counteract any obvious effect of rhythm running simultaneously through all the parts' (Parry, *Music of the Seventeenth Century*). It seems to be a case of melodic purity against general rhythm. If we want melodic purity, as the polyphonic writers did, then we must adopt their syllabic arrangement; if we want general rhythm, then we shall keep to our own arrangement.

Coincident with this change of view has been a different sense of the relative importance of the up and down beats. The strong beat of the Plain-song writers, and probably of the Madrigalists as well, was the up beat, or *arsis*; the weak one was the down beat, or *thesis*. This has been definitely reversed, with the consequence that we are now liable to beat in time, in self-contained bars, without any true sense of rhythm. But with the acceptance of the up beat as the chief beat, or beat of impulse, music *connects back* over the bar, and becomes vital and organic.* Incidentally, it

---

* The tendency to associate musical impulse with an upward movement may quite possibly have had a very subtle influence upon musicians and their art. For the upward movement suggests a lifting quality, a spiritual urge, much as Gothic architecture soared into the heavens. Whereas insistence on the downward stress, by no extreme analogy, seems to bring music to earth, towards the physical. Plain-song as representing the one, and the Dance as representing the other, may well be contrasted here. The former with its unstressed *legato* is almost the antithesis of the latter, where percussive, *marcato* effects are predominant. And there can be little doubt which is the more spiritual manifestation.

may also be regarded as a justification for the passage from Morley already quoted, and this one which is similar:

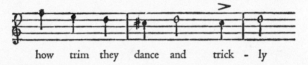

how   trim   they   dance   and   trick - ly

There is a great deal more in this than at first glance appears, and, if worked out to the full, it might well be the very foundation of a true philosophy of rhythm, a subject which is fraught with difficulty, as the writer is only too well aware.

Build of Madrigals

MADRIGALS are built in successive sections (or blocks) of imitative passages. A line or so of the lyric is taken and fitted to a theme which is discussed between the voices. This is succeeded by similar treatment of the next line of the lyric, and so on. Though the best Madrigals show a certain unity throughout, each section presents some fresh idea verbally and musically. This generally calls for contrast in performance, most often by a change of tone, and in this way the build of the Madrigal is indicated and variety gained. Sometimes these sections of imitations come to a full stop, are self-contained, as it were, and have no connexion with the succeeding section. Performance in this case calls for no comment. Sometimes, however, the voices of the one section are made to flow into the succeeding section, so that there is a sort of dovetailing between them. When this is so, care should generally be taken that the contrast of tone is in the new entries only. The individuality of each imitative section should remain to the end of the section, no matter where the voices drop out. An example (p. 87) will make this clear.

The section 'Where we are drest for this short comedy' is preceded by a section to the words 'Our mothers' wombs the tiring houses be'. These sections are closely allied in spirit. Mystery and restraint should characterize the performance of both. But with the next section, 'Heav'n the judicious, &c.', an altogether different strain is arrived at. The sense of the preceding was *p* or *pp*; this must be *f*. But the *f* must only be emphasized in the new entries: first, by the second soprano (bar 4), then the first soprano (bar 5), and then the bass (bar 7). Till these entries are reached the voices should be subdued. The tendency in such a passage is for *all* the voices to follow the *f* lead, when it first occurs, and sing *f* too, seemingly encouraged by the conductor, who has to apply himself mainly to the sense of the new entries.*

What is our Life—ORLANDO GIBBONS

* The *crescendo* at bar 6 in the alto is marked for the rise of the phrase; that at bar 7 in the tenor is marked because the tenor here represents the bass of the passage, and it would sound weak at this point if the melodic expression only were considered in the tenor, and a *diminuendo* made. It is perhaps worth while to remark that the parts of the first and second soprano sound well sung *f*,

In this example the contrast between the sections is from *piano* to *forte*; so that there is no danger of the *f* entries being obscured. When the contrast is from *forte* to *piano* there certainly is a danger, but nevertheless the individuality of the sections should be kept. A previous example from Bennet shows this contrast from *forte* to *piano*:

Thyrsis, sleepest thou—BENNET

Sometimes, however, it is possible and (wherever it can be done) advisable to modify the *forte* of a voice which overlaps a *piano* section, as in 'Lightly she Whipped' (p. 89). Here the first section is *forte* to the words, 'Making the woods proud', &c. At the point of overlapping there is not the slightest objection to the second soprano singing very softly because, although the words belong to the *forte* section, the music is entirely insignificant of it. With the 'Thyrsis' example the case was different. For the

while the lower parts are sung *p* because the second soprano forms a good bass to the first soprano. These two parts could exist by themselves as satisfactory part writing; if they could not, the expression of the passage would have to be modified as at the end of the tenor part.

Lightly she Whipp'd—MUNDY

phrase in the soprano is the phrase characteristic of the section. It could not be sung truthfully *piano* or with any other expression than that of energetic reproach.

The necessity for contrasting sections is so great that, when both sections are naturally *forte*, a *piano* should sometimes be made immediately before the second group of *f* entries merely for the purposes of securing a contrast, as in 'Sweet Honey-sucking Bees' (p. 90).

It should be remarked that the start of sections is perhaps their most *effective* point—the point where they tell most; for the listener is entirely fresh to the matter then, and is therefore particularly open to its impression. For this reason one should aim at defining the *start* of sections as clearly as possible.

N

Sweet Honey-sucking Bees—WILBYE

We might refer here to an erstwhile prevalent notion that there is no place in polyphonic music for *crescendos, diminuendos,* or any varied expression whatsoever, save perhaps an occasional strongly contrasted change from *f* to *p.* As though it were possible to deny music its nature because it happens to be a few centuries old!* We must take stand beside the late

---

* It is, perhaps, worth noticing that expression marks (called the Romanian signs) the equivalent of our own signs of *accel., rit., cres., dim., p., f.,* &c., were used in the performance of Gregorian music as far back as the eighth century. We are apt to think that what we call 'expression' is a modern feature of music, and it is a little chastening to know that the essential modifications of time and tone, upon which expressive performance depends, were in use so long ago. In view of these ancient signs we shall probably be not far wrong in assuming that the Elizabethans (some

Mr. W. S. Rockstro when he expresses himself on Madrigal singing in the following suggestive passage: 'Changes of tone', he says, 'embracing every shade of difference between *ff* and *ppp*, and introduced, sometimes by the most delicate possible gradations, and sometimes, in strongly-marked contrast, will be continually demanded, both by the character of the music and the sense of the words; and, remembering how earnestly Morley insists upon 'varietie',* the student will be prepared to learn that *ritardandi* and *accelerandi* will be scarcely less frequently brought into requisition. Nevertheless, strict mechanical precision must be secured at any cost. The slightest uncertainty, either of intonation, or of rhythm, will suffice to ruin everything; and to draw the line fairly between intensity of expression and technical perfection is not always an easy matter. There is, indeed, only one way of overcoming the difficulty. To imagine Damon regulating his lovelorn ditty by the tick of a metronome would be absurd. The place of the metronome, therefore, must be supplied by a conductor, capable of fully sympathizing, either with Damon's woes, or Daphne's fond delights, but wholly incapable of showing the least indulgence to his singers, who must learn to obey the rise and fall of his baton, though it move but a hair's breadth in either direction.'

Character

TRY to give character not only to the Madrigal as a whole but to each phrase. In works of the best composers the words supply the key to the emotion. But they do more than this. The actual structure and sequence of words, phonetically, influence the expression of the music to a very great degree; and beautiful musical effects are often realized merely through observing an ofttimes subtle force which the words exercise on the music. For instance, the short vowels are suited for light, *staccato* effects;

800 years later) sung their music with a very fair degree of expression; perhaps with as much or more than some of us think worth while to bestow upon it nowadays.

    * 'If, therefore, you will (sing) in this kind you must possess yourself with an amorous humour (for in no (singing) shall you prove admirable except you put on, and possess yourself wholly with the vein (of the song)) so that you must in your (singing) be wavering like the wind, sometime wanton, sometime drooping, sometime grave and stadie, otherwhile effeminat, . . . showing the uttermost of your varietie, and the more varietie you shew the better shall you please.'—From *A Plaine and Easie Introduction.*

not so the long vowels. *Marcato* effects suit the long vowels; but seldom short *staccato*. In Wilbye's 'Sweet Honey-sucking Bees', on the words 'pinks and violets' there is a note to each syllable, and in one generally admirable edition of the Madrigal each note is directed to be sung *staccato*, evidently with the idea of introducing delicacy and lightness at this point, in itself entirely desirable. But the word 'violets' does not lend itself to a separation of its syllables. In the first place the central part of the word is quite liquid; the 'i' naturally flows into the 'o', and the 'o' into the 'l'. In the second place the vowels 'i' and 'o' are long vowels. So instead of getting lightness on the word by singing the syllables *staccato* the word is simply denatured, and the effect forced and heavy.

In singing, the natural features of words may be exaggerated, but not changed (unless under exceptional circumstances). If, when spoken, syllables are naturally connected (as in the words 'fair⌢O⌢ri⌢a⌢na'), sing them connected. If syllables are naturally distinct (as in such a series of words as 'sweet and kind') sing them distinctly, and even detach them into frank *staccato* if it agrees with the sentiment to be expressed.

Perhaps no two different phrases are expressed in exactly the same manner. Infinite variety of phrasing is not only possible but inevitable, and, only when we have considered the mechanical structure of the verbal and musical elements, and the inner sentiment of both (which may be expected to correspond), shall we succeed in giving *character* to our singing.

Elizabethan Pronunciation

THE Elizabethans sometimes seem to put an extra syllable into words, compared with present usage. These extra syllables must be distinctly sung, as in:

the   right - e - ous for - sak - en

and the words should never be approximated to its modern form in which elision has occurred.

Occasionally also the Elizabethan accenting of a word is different to ours—e.g. the word 'July', which was stressed on the first syllable and not the second. Thus in Morley's 4-part Madrigal, 'April is in my mistress' face', we find:

and   Ju - ly in her eyes   hath . .   place

and the phrase is rightly accented as above, in accordance with the musical principle of accenting the first of a group of relatively quick notes.

Fa-la Refrains of Ballets, &c.

IN these refrains broad fah lah lah should not be sung throughout. The 'ah' must be modified to suit the style of the music, which is light and tripping, not heavy and deliberate. Something like fah luhl luhl (like 'u' in 'dull') should be sung on the shorter notes, keeping the broader 'fah' and 'lah' for the longer accented notes. Thus the following example would be sung:

See the Shepherds' Queen—TOMKINS

Fah   luhl luhl luhl luhl luhl luhl luhl luhl lah
(not Fah   lah   lah   lah lah   lah   lah   lah   lah lah)

These 'luhls' should, moreover, be sung so that the vowel, which in this way gives a sort of sting to the 'l', is only heard for a moment just at the start of each note, the sound being continued by the 'l'. Thus the interstices of the vowel *staccatos* are filled up, and a very delicate mixture of *staccato* and *legato* results.* Put into notation, it would be something like

Fah   luh - l   luh - l   luh - l

* If the singer has any difficulty in realizing this effect, let him sing a continuous 'l', as it were, allowing the tongue to fall just for a moment at the start of each note.

This smothered tone of the 'l' is frequently very effective; as also that of 'n' and 'ng' and even 'm'. It is not suggested that the final sound of 'l', &c., is suitable for sustained singing, but only for fairly quick notes and for elastic springing effects.

The singer should not take it (from this modifying of fa la) that the pronunciation of vowel sounds may be modified to suit the music. It is only on such nonsense syllables as fa la that any great modification can be made, for the reason that there is next to no received pronunciation of these syllables. The singer must be ever so wary of altering the received pronunciations. Ludicrous caricatures are sometimes to be heard when singers try to get what they call more *tone* (!) on words. I have heard a solo-singer deliberately sing 'aitch' for 'each'. When I remonstrated, he justi-fied himself by saying that he could get no tone on 'e'. This, of course, is exceptional, but I mention it to show that there is some occasion for insisting on purity of pronunciation.

Transposition

IT is quite permissible to transpose a Madrigal to a pitch where greater effectiveness is secured. This can easily be done with an unaccompanied song, though often, unfortunately, when instrumental accompaniment is concerned it is impossible. It is only by experiment that what is un-doubtedly the best key for the song can be decided upon; and it is strange how a certain pitch will obviously suit it, satisfying both its nature and the particular vocal capacity of the choir, though another choir might find another pitch more suitable. Thus a gay song will often gain by being transposed up a little, and a grave one may be better if transposed down. Moreover, it is undoubtedly best to make things as easy for the voices as possible so that they do not seem to be strained. The main care must be that the Sopranos shall not have too high notes to sing, nor the Basses too low ones to give a sonorous ground tone. But the voices named in any good edition should generally be adhered to. For instance, when the lowest part is assigned to the tenor voice, it should not be sung by the basses.

Speed

FORMALLY there is more in a word than a note. And expressively it is fair to say that there is more personality in a word than in a note; it means more. This has already been indicated on a preceding page. Hence there is perhaps something in this: that if vocal music be regarded primarily as a vehicle for verbal utterance it will tend to be taken more slowly than if it be looked upon rather in the light of instrumental music, with the words of little account. For words take a certain time to make their effect and cannot be unduly hurried, or they will lose both definition and fervency. On the other hand, instrumental music can be taken relatively quickly while retaining its clarity. Indeed, if it be taken too slow it becomes wearisome and does not connect up. Therefore I think we may say that vocal music is of a slower order of speed than instrumental music. In other words, a song, particularly a highly expressive one, can be sung more slowly than the music by itself can be played. And so we are apt to find that a conductor who is used mainly to orchestral music will take choral music too fast—not allowing the words to make their due point and significance, while a choral conductor, who is used to dwell lovingly on words, will be apt to take instrumental music too slow.

There is perhaps, now, a danger of singing old music too quick, but it is quite certain that formerly it was sung much too slow. This was due to the crotchet being taken as the unit beat, as in most modern practice, whereas the minim nearly always represents the beat in Madrigals. It can be easily seen when this is not the case. In a slow Madrigal the ♩ may be about 50–60 M.M.; in a quick one 100 M.M. or more. But no rule can be given, and it is only by experiment, or intuition, that an approximately right tempo can be fixed. A good rule is to sing Madrigalian music as quickly as you can, while preserving the spirit of the song in question.

Never think of notes as single, but always as grouped in twos and threes. Gather as much of the music as you conveniently can under each beat. It will considerably affect speed.

This also has a bearing upon the matter: the more you put into music—

though expression should never take an exaggerated form and should always be within the bounds of good taste—the slower you can take it; and vice versa. A superficial rendering, to be endurable, must move at a relatively quick pace.

Conclusion

IN the foregoing pages our chief concern has been to dwell upon the need for individual, almost competitive expression in each part, and we have tried to show how nearly every particular of Madrigal expression may be reduced to the principles of melodic expression. At rehearsal, therefore, the conductor will pay great attention to seeing that the unit melody, or theme, of each group of imitations is well sung; and the quickest method of study is to let all the voices sing the theme together, at some pitch at which they can all join comfortably. If this unit theme is well sung, the greater and certainly the most vital part of the expression has been achieved. The difficulty of good ensemble is, of course, not to be underrated; but good ensemble without melodic detail is, literally, the body without life.

The success of all art, whether creative or interpretive, must reside in the simple query, 'Is it appropriate?' The few indications for Madrigal performance set down in the preceding pages are probably true enough, but they must never be applied without thought or at least without feeling. Every issue must be judged for itself. The artist takes nothing for granted. He is ever open to determine afresh. But he knows full well that when contradictions seem to occur, it is not because they really exist, but because it is impossible to focus all considerations in some single rule.

Much of this little book is about technical matters only, but the first thing in art is to be a good workman. Spiritual considerations can almost be left to themselves if technical foundations are well and truly laid. What is lacking in many artists is not sensibility or imagination, but simply efficient workmanship without which the soul cannot manifest itself in adequate form. A feeble, shaky body is not likely to be of much use for great deeds either in art or life.

Finally, it must be said that though this book may have an analytical interest and be helpful in supplying certain lines of study, it does not nor cannot touch essentials which can only be supplied by the singer himself, viz. an instinct for rhythmic flow, a sense of proportion which will give as it were a classic beauty to variations of time and force, and what can only be called the quality of inspiration which, seeing 'into the life of things', will unconsciously modify even those variations, transcending purely formal perfection.

APPENDIX
*A Note on the Modal System**

EVERY piece of music, to be intelligible, must be constructed upon some definite series of notes; upon some scale or mode. Madrigals are constructed upon one or other of the twelve Church modes, from which our modern major and minor scales were evolved.† These modes, when untransposed, consist of notes which are identical with the notes of our modern scale of C major. The following is a table of the modes:

Table of the Church Modes

(The notes of the Authentic Mode are indicated above the stave; those of the Plagal‡ below the stave)

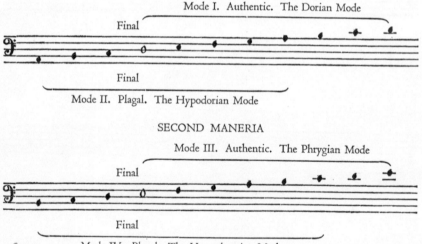

FIRST MANERIA §

Mode I. Authentic. The Dorian Mode

Mode II. Plagal. The Hypodorian Mode

SECOND MANERIA

Mode III. Authentic. The Phrygian Mode

Mode IV. Plagal. The Hypophrygian Mode

* For a further account of the polyphonic scale system see Preface to vol. i, *Euterpe*, by Mr. J. A. Fuller Maitland, published by the Oriana Madrigal Society; also the Preface to vol. iii on *Modes and Keys* by Mr. G. E. P. Arkwright. Perhaps the best book to give the clue to *all* matters connected with polyphonic music is Mr. R. O. Morris's *Contrapuntal Technique in the Sixteenth Century* (Oxford University Press).

† This, indeed, is the great peculiarity of Madrigals. A Madrigal might be shortly defined as a piece of unaccompanied secular, vocal music, based upon the modal scale system.

‡ The word Plagal means derived—derived from the notes of the authentic mode.

§ The complete series of notes (from A to D) shows the mixture of the first and second modes. Sometimes a melody ranged through this whole series of notes, in which case it was said to be in the first and second modes *mixed*.

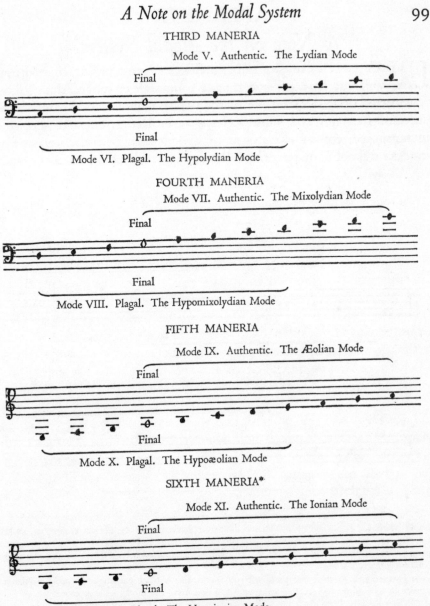

THIRD MANERIA

Mode V. Authentic. The Lydian Mode

Mode VI. Plagal. The Hypolydian Mode

FOURTH MANERIA

Mode VII. Authentic. The Mixolydian Mode

Mode VIII. Plagal. The Hypomixolydian Mode

FIFTH MANERIA

Mode IX. Authentic. The Æolian Mode

Mode X. Plagal. The Hypoæolian Mode

SIXTH MANERIA*

Mode XI. Authentic. The Ionian Mode

Mode XII. Plagal. The Hypoionian Mode

* It will be noticed that the *maneria* starting on F (with final B) is omitted. The old musicians did not use the modes of this maneria on account of impurity in their construction. The Eleventh Ionian mode, as noted above is, of course, none other than our modern major mode.

It will be seen that modes I, III, V, VII, IX, and XI are arrived at by taking each of the notes of the scale of C major as a final (with the exception of the note B) and continuing the series of notes of C major. It will also be seen that the modes go in pairs : modes I and II together, III and IV together, and so on. They are so grouped because melodies written in either of the modes of a pair (or *maneria*) end on the same final. The difference between a melody written in the first and a melody written in the second mode is one of range. A melody in the first mode, for instance, will lie within the octave above from D, subject to certain licences. A melody in the second mode will lie within the octave from A, a fourth below the final D. The melody must end on D, however, in both modes.

Though the use of the same final begets a similarity between the Authentic and the Plagal modes, as the first and second of *each pair* is called, yet the musical impression that they convey is by no means the same. Every mode has certain characteristics. So much so that the old musicians called the first mode *Modus Gravis*, or the Grave Mode; the second mode *Modus Tristis*, or the Mournful Mode: that is to say, melodies written in the first mode were liable to be of a grave character, in the second of a mournful character, and so on. These differences of effect were brought about by the different *relation* of the notes of the modes to the final or tonic note.

This, then, was the material, and a sufficiently varied one, which the Madrigal composer had to dispose of in the composition of his Madrigals. For his melody it was perfect, infinitely more perfect than the material of our modern scales, inasmuch as it was more comprehensive. For his harmony it was unfortunately imperfect; and in combining his melodies, in the process of composition, certain alterations in the modes were required, which to a large extent cancelled the characteristics of the modes (wherein lay the perfection of the system), and indeed eventually destroyed their characteristics altogether. Thus in harmonic cadences a leading note or note a half-tone below the final note of the scale is almost a necessity.

The unsatisfactory nature of such a progression as that in the next example, without the C sharp (employing only the true notes of the first mode), will be immediately perceived. But with the sharp the cadence seems natural and correct. Also, if at the close of a phrase a minor chord ensued from the use of the true notes of the mode, it was altered into a major chord by a sharp.

These and other alterations were summed up under certain rules, called the rules of Musica Ficta; but as a matter of fact composers did not stop here, and eventually, for expression purposes, prefixed sharps and flats to the true notes of the modes pretty much as they pleased.

The mode in which a Madrigal is written may be ascertained by observing (1) the Bass note in the last bar; this will give the final of the mode. Then see (2) whether the mode has been transposed. If there is no sharp or flat in the signature* (as in the modern key of C major), the mode has not been transposed, and the Bass note will be the true final. If there is sharp or flat for signature, the mode has been transposed, and the series of notes (starting from the transposed final) must be identified with a similar series of notes in the untransposed modes. This will give the true final. Whether it is the authentic or plagal form of the *maneria* must then be found (3). If the high voice parts, i.e. the Tenor and Soprano parts, lie mostly between the final and the octave above, the mode will be authentic. If the range of these parts lies mostly between a 4th below and a 5th above the final, it will be plagal. The compass may often be found to exceed these limits by a note or two; but the general lie of the part will (as a rule) clearly indicate whether it is authentic or plagal. Thus, if the last chord of a Madrigal is noted:

* The only signature which the polyphonic writers themselves admitted was that of one flat or two flats, i.e. a transposition of any scale to a 5th below (one flat), or a 4th above (two flats). *They never transposed to the sharp side.* No sharp signature is to be found in any polyphonic music. But in modern editions of Madrigals, &c., any transposition is made—to the flat or *to the sharp side*, in order to suit the best pitch for singing.

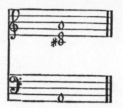

(without any sharp or flat in the signature), the Bass note A is a true final, and the mode is either IX or X. If the range of the Tenor (or Soprano) is from A to A (approximately), it will be in the authentic 9th mode. If the range is from E to E (approximately), it will be in the plagal 10th mode.

Again, if the last chord is noted :

(with B flat in the signature), the mode is a transposed mode; so A will not be the true final. This transposed series :

agrees, as regards the sequence of intervals, with the 3rd mode :

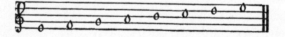

i.e. the mode has been transposed down a fifth, and the Madrigal will be either in the 3rd or 4th mode according as the compass of the Tenor or Soprano is between A and A or E and E.

Again, if the last chord of a Madrigal is

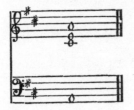

A is not the true final. The mode has been transposed. This transposed
series :

agrees with

so that the Madrigal will be either in the 7th or 8th mode as is settled
from the range of the Tenor or Soprano part. The above transposition is
purely a modern transposition (v. note, p. 101). Sometimes it may happen
that an 'improving' editor, seeing certain accidentals appear in a piece,
thinks he is justified in incorporating them in the signature. For instance,
in Weelkes's three-part Madrigal, 'The Nightingale' (from *Ayres or
Fantasticke Spirites*, 1608), there is no key-signature in the original. It is
written for two Sopranos and Alto. The compass of the Sopranos lies
between G and G. The final is G ; therefore the piece is in the seventh
mode. Oliphant, in editing this Madrigal, transposed it up a tone, in
which case the key-signature should have been two sharps; but he placed
three sharps, and even went to the length of sharpening the seventh of the
mode throughout, though it is only sometimes sharpened in the original.
The effect of this is to alter the mode (and consequently the character of
the piece) entirely. Not only this, but he altered the syllabic distribution
of the words and re-wrote the music in places. Such editing is altogether
unwarrantable. Obvious misprints in the original should of course be corrected; but beyond this the editor should not go. He should print the
composition exactly as it stands or, at any rate, leave it clear how it stood.

A Note on Ayres

THE modal system did not debar harmonized song, any more than the modern key system debars polyphony. Now that we have established harmonic relationships, it is as easy for us to harmonize a modal melody as a modern melody; only we shall probably destroy the character of the former as a modal melody by doing so. Nevertheless, before the advent of the key system, the modal system was inseparable from polyphony; because under the modal system harmony was not understood in the sense of definite key relationship, involving modulation. In reality composers were engaged in defining harmony through polyphony; and once harmony had been defined the modal system automatically disappeared. For melodic purposes the composer was sure of his ground in dealing with the modes. He could keep to the natural notes of the mode he was writing in with perfect propriety as regards his melody; or modify the notes if he chose, still thoroughly understanding his position. But he could not keep to the notes of the mode for his harmony. Almost from the first he recognized that he could not combine parts without chromatically altering the notes of the modes. Such alteration would only become systematized by slow degrees; and it was not till the composer had so modified the modes, bringing all the twelve modes to the common denominator of the modern major and minor scales in his search for a sure harmonic foothold, that he could eventually deal with his harmonic material with the same assurance as he had all along been able to deal with his melodic material. It would have been the same to the composer, from the point of view of his melody, whether he had to deal with the ecclesiastical modes or the modern scales. His position would have been satisfactory in either case. But from the point of view of his harmony he could never have a certain method of harmonization till the modes were discarded. Modes were a sufficient guide for his polyphony; but key is the only sufficient guide for harmonization. It is true that his instinct for harmony served the polyphonic composer right well in the majority of cases. The vagueness and indecision as to harmony that may be observed in polyphonic compositions is a thing which many prize rather than condemn. The fact, however, remains that this vagueness implies that harmonic relationships had not been firmly grasped, and that, therefore, at this period, the polyphonic method was the only method that composers could employ satisfactorily. If the parts of a polyphonic composition are not melodious and seem to be based upon harmony rather than polyphony, it is because the skill and fancy of the composer failed, or that he did not wish to apply it, not that he was working on the principle of harmonization.*

From various causes our English Madrigals date at quite the end of the polyphonic period, or rather at what may be called the period of transition between the modal system and the modern key system. Properly speaking, there was transition going on all the time under the modal system. But about the beginning of the seventeenth century the modal system had been strained to its furthest limits. So that, without knowing it, composers often wrote in nothing short of modern keys, though in most of their compositions, particularly in the more extended form of the Madrigal proper, the modal element is quite apparent. For this reason it is going too far to say that our English madrigalian writings *must* be polyphonic. We may even expect to find them exhibit some overlapping of the polyphonic and monodic styles. Yet we shall not be going far wrong when we say that there is no such thing as a subordinate part in a Madrigal, Ballet, or Choral Ayre.

We are in no difficulty in substantiating this in the case of Madrigals and Ballets, since imitation is a constant feature in both. These can be classed as polyphonic without hesitation. Our difficulty is with Ayres. In the face of their title we seem bound to admit that the Ayre implies an Air or principal part and that, therefore, the Ayre must be classed as monodic. Chappell, indeed, in his preface to Dowland's *First Book of Ayres*, 1597 (Mus. Antiquarian Society's publication, 1844), calls them 'harmonized songs' without more ado. But that is an injustice. They are very much more than this as we understand harmonized song nowadays. The term could only be applied to the last one in the book (No. 21), and perhaps to No. 6, 'Now, O now, I needs must part'.

There is evidently a very general idea that Ballets and Ayres are the equivalent of modern part (or harmonized) songs. In the article, 'Part Song', in Grove's Dictionary, the writer refers to the Ballets of Morley

---

* The term *polyphony* is almost exclusively associated with the music of the modal system, probably from the fact that harmonization was impossible under it.

as including 'perfect examples of the part song as we now understand it', and as 'maintaining their position . . . by reason of their crisp, well-marked rhythm, and simple pleasing melody'.

We must contradict this, even in the interests of proper performance. If Ayres and Ballets were merely harmonized song, the accompanying parts would have to be sung much softer than the melody in order to allow the melody to be brought into prominence, but there is scarcely ever justification for such a procedure.

Of the music of this transitional period the truth seems to be that, though the monodic style was within the grasp of its composers, it was only so to a certain extent and could only be displayed in such revolutionary compositions as *Ayres for Solo Voice and Lute*; whereas in compositions written in vocal parts they were more or less bound by the old traditions and framed them upon the polyphonic style. There is nothing improbable about this in the case of *Ayres in parts*. For they have a direct prototype in the Old English Song, which was certainly of a polyphonic nature though of plain composition; and continuity would likely be sustained as long as polyphonic methods lasted. That at this period the polyphonic and the monodic styles were used side by side, and even by the same musicians, there is no manner of doubt. Morley wrote his *First Book of Aires, or little Short Songs to sing and play to the Lute with the Base Viol*, as well as Madrigals and Motets in which he employs the highest ingenuity as regards polyphony.

It remains to be seen whether Ayres *in parts*, such as were printed from 1597 onwards, were in the first place conceived chorally or whether they are in reality compositions for solo voice and lute. If the former, they are likely to be polyphonic. If the latter, they may well be monodic.

That Ayres *in parts** were conceived chorally may be argued from the fact that Dowland says his *First Book* is 'so made, that all the parts together or *either of them severally* may be sung to the lute, orpharion or viol di gambo'; from which we may infer (1) that he placed no great stress on the superior melody of any one part (as he would have done if he had framed them for a solo voice), and (2) that if either of the parts could be 'sung severally' with good effect, the combination of 'all the parts together' would produce a better.

Directly opposed to this is Campion's assertion that the Ayres of his

---

* Nearly always *four* parts, S.A.T.B.

Two Bookes of Ayres (undated, but probably 1613) 'were for the most part fram'd at first for one Voyce with the Lute or Violl'. But I think this is quite exceptional, proved even by his drawing attention to the fact; and (as we may expect from the admission) the Ayres in these particular Books are quite of the nature of *Solo* Ayres and have not the choral characteristics that Dowland's, Pilkington's, or Ford's Ayres have.

It is also possible to argue that Ayres in parts were primarily intended as Solo compositions from the fact that all Ayres have lute accompaniment.* This accompaniment always appears under the highest part, showing, perhaps, that this part was specially looked upon as the air. But if it was so, we see in such a passage as the following,

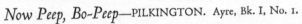

Now Peep, Bo-Peep—PILKINGTON. Ayre, Bk. I, No. 1.

* Which gives the gist of the three lower voices only, from which we may assume that the lute accompaniment was not intended for use if the Ayre was sung as a choral composition (for in this

how empty and meaningless the air part would be if performed by lute and solo voice alone. The passage has no point except as a choral passage. In other words, the air, if the upper part be taken as the air, cannot be satisfactorily detached from the other parts, i.e. it cannot exist apart as a tune. It would, of course, be exaggerating to say that the treble part can never stand as a tune by itself. In many cases it can, and in the case of 'Now, O now, I needs must part' (Dowland), did exist as a popular tune under the name of 'The Frog Galliard' (see Chappell's Preface already quoted); and the effect of the upper part given only with lute accompaniment would be very pleasing. It is possible to concede this without damaging our case that an Ayre is polyphonic rather than monodic. It need only prove that Elizabethan composers were extremely skilful in part writing.

There is still another reason for holding that Ayres in parts could not offer any certain expression of the monodic principle, something where the song would be so distinct from the accompanying parts that it could be called harmonized song without reservation. With Ayres for solo voice and lute the contrast between melody and accompaniment is arrived at by the nature of the accompaniment itself. The lute is almost of necessity a harmonic instrument; any writing for the lute appears to be harmonic, even though it may have a polyphonic basis. This was seen in our example from Pilkington. But the voice is essentially a melodic instrument, and in some degree must always be treated melodically, even in combination.* Hence, unless the melody of the principal voice can be made much more striking than the melody of the accompanying parts, there will only be a very uncertain expression of harmonized song. But in proportion as the principal melody is more striking, so will the expression of harmonized song become clearer. Now, without wishing to underrate its significance, it may be said that Elizabethan melody was not particularly striking. It was simple and undeveloped compared to later melody. It was a type that had been evolved

case there would have been no reasons for omitting the highest voice from the lute part). The lute accompaniment does not seem to be essential to Ayres in parts at all (though it almost invariably goes with them), but, together with the highest part, seems to constitute a sort of *arrangement* of the choral Ayre, so that the composition could be used in this way if desired, forming a precedent to the present-day fashion of arranging compositions in every conceivable shape and form.

* In choral composition the monodic principle is seldom carried to extreme limits. There may, of course, be a distinct principal melody in the upper part and distinct accompaniment in the lower parts ; but it is only in instrumental accompaniment (on lute, harp, piano, &c.) that the very baldest methods of accompaniment are reached in the shape of note repetitions, arpeggios, alberti basses, &c.

through polyphony, or at any rate had been largely influenced by poly-phony, splendid for the purposes of polyphonic composition as a whole, giving it unapproached strength and dignity,* but only moderately salient as melody, apart from its context. It was thus possible to use it in several parts at once, so that each part was melodious after the polyphonic fashion, but no part necessarily predominated. We may even say that the Eliza-bethans had not the means of contrasting *vocal* parts to any great extent, though they certainly had arrived at the idea of harmony as an independent principle, if they chose to employ it as such.

But, without attempting to decide *why*, in point of history, choral Ayres should be polyphonic rather than monodic, we have only to look at the Ayres themselves for assurance that it is so. In Nos. 3, 4, 5, and 18, especially 18, of Dowland's First Book, for instance, we should scarcely recognize any special air were it not that in the highest part repetition of the words is avoided and the melody is a little less cut up. In No. 20 it is impossible to distinguish which part is even meant for the air, while in Nos. 9, 14, and 16 there is very near approach to the imitative Madrigal style. Almost the same features are to be observed in Pilkington's Ayres, which, together with the Ayres of Dowland, are those with which the Madrigal singer is particularly concerned.†

Further, independent rhythms, i.e. rhythms in which neither the ex-tremes of rhythm nor their musical accents coincide, are common in Ayres.

---

* A polyphonic composition appeals in much the same way as Norman architecture by its splendid effect of *mass*.

Architects tell us that the Normans wasted their material ; that their buildings would have stood with half the stone. The polyphonic composers were equally profuse with their material. They delighted in compositions in many parts ; in making every part equally melodious ; in lading their compositions with fugue and canonical device, which is often (it must be confessed) wasted for its own sake. The revolutionary Campion evidently felt this when he ridiculed those 'who to appeare the more deepe and singular in their judgement will admit no musicke but that which is long, intricate, bated with fuge and chained with syncopation'. Yet, by getting *mass* into their work, the polyphonic composers sufficiently justified their methods.

There is further similarity between polyphonic composition and Norman architecture. Both, in some measure, typify art in the making. Norman decoration is manifestly rugged, even to the point of uncouthness. Polyphony has few of the graces of expression that came at a later period. But for this reason both strike strong and sturdy. There is no smoothing down till the strength has gone ; none of the fine polish, or the perfect regularity that seems to be everything but the essential.

† In his *Plaine and Easie Introduction to Practicall Musicke*, Morley, after talking of Ballete (or Ballets), says, 'These and all other kinds of light musick, saving the Madrigal, are by a general name called Aires' ; so that the term Ayre was exceedingly comprehensive.

This independence is often joined to imitative writing, which still more surely equalizes the melodic value of the parts. But the mere fact of coincident rhythms being the exception rather than the rule is, in itself, sufficient evidence of the polyphonic nature of Ayres.

To sum up as regards Ayres. The more serious-minded composers of Ayres, and those who, in some measure, had the technical resources of the period at their command, such as Dowland and Pilkington, wrote in a style but little removed from the polyphonic style of the Madrigal proper— due allowance being made for the characteristics of the Ayre as a straight-forward song form; while such composers as Ford, who were evidently less skilled in the art of music, though full of musical feeling, wrote in a style less related to polyphony, though still showing its influence.

A List of Madrigals and Ballets

published during what is generally known as the Elizabethan period

BYRD (WILLIAM)
Psalmes, Sonets, and Songs of Sadnes and Pietie made into Musicke of five parts. 1588.
Songs of Sundrie Natures, composed into Musicke of 3, 4, 5, and 6 parts. 1589.
Psalmes, Songs and Sonnets, some solemn others joyfull. Fit for Voyces or Viols of 3, 4, 5, and 6 parts. 1611.

MORLEY (THOMAS)
Canzonets, or Little Short Songs to three voyces. 1593.
Madrigalls to foure voyces. 1594.
The First Booke of Ballets to five voyces. 1595.
The First Book of Canzonets to two voyces. 1595.
Canzonets or Little Short Aers to five and 6 voyces. 1597.
The Triumphs of Oriana to five and 6 voyces. 1601.

MUNDY (JOHN)
Songs and Psalmes, composed into 3, 4, and 5 parts. 1594.

WEELKES (THOMAS)
Madrigals to 3, 4, 5, and 6 voyces. 1597.
Ballets and Madrigals to 5 voyces, with one to 6 voyces. 1598.
Madrigals of 5 parts. 1600.
Madrigals of 6 parts. 1600.
Ayeres or Phantasticke Spirites for three voyces. 1608.

KIRBYE (GEORGE)
The first set of English Madrigals to 4, 5 and 6 voyces. 1597.

HOLBORNE (WILLIAM)
Sixe short Aers or Canzonets to three voyces. 1597.

CAVENDISH (MICHAEL)
Ayres for Four Voyces. 1598.

WILBYE (JOHN)
The First Set of English madrigals to 3, 4, 5, and 6 voices. 1598.
The Second Set of Madrigals to 3, 4, 5, and 6 parts. 1609.

FARNABY (GILES)
Canzonets to foure voyces. 1598.

FARMER (JOHN)
The First Set of English Madrigals to Foure Voyces. 1599.

BENNET (JOHN)
Madrigalls to Foure Voyces. 1599.

CARLTON (RICHARD)
Madrigals to Five Voyces. 1601.

EAST (MICHAEL)
Madrigals to 3, 4, and 5 parts. 1604.
The Second Set of Madrigals to 3, 4, and 5 parts. 1606.
The Third Set of Bookes wherein are Pastorals, Anthemes, Neapolitaines, Fancies, and Madrigals to 5 and 6 parts. 1610.
The Fourth Set of Bookes, wherein are Anthemes, etc., to 4, 5, and 6 parts. 1619.

BATESON (THOMAS)
The First Set of English Madrigals of 3, 4, 5, and 6 voices. 1604.
The Second Set of English Madrigals of 3, 4, 5, and 6 parts. 1618.

GREAVES (THOMAS)
Madrigalls for five Voyces. 1604.

ALISON (RICHARD)
An Houres Recreation in Musicke. 1606.

JONES (ROBERT)
The First Set of Madrigals of 3, 4, 5, 6, 7, 8 parts. 1607.

YOULL (HENRY)
Canzonets to three voyces. 1608.

GIBBONS (ORLANDO)
The First Set of Madrigals and Mottets of 5 parts. 1612.

WARD (JOHN)
The First Set of English Madrigals to 3, 4, 5, and 6 parts. 1613.

PILKINGTON (FRANCIS)
The First Set of Madrigals and Pastorals of 3, 4, and 5 parts. 1613.
The Second Set of Madrigals and Pastorals of 3, 4, 5, and 6 parts. 1624.

LICHFIELD (HENRY)
The First Set of Madrigals of 5 parts. 1613.

VAUTOR (THOMAS)
The First Set : Being Songs of divers Ayres and Natures. 1619.

TOMKINS (THOMAS)
Songs of 3, 4, 5, and 6 parts. 1622.

N.B.—These volumes, consisting of some 600 Madrigals in all, have been reprinted by Dr. E. H. Fellowes in *The English Madrigal School* (Stainer and Bell).
Richard Edwards's *Madrigals to 4 voyces* (1560), though falling outside the main body of our English Madrigals, may also be mentioned here.

A List of Choral Ayres
published during the Elizabethan period

DOWLAND (JOHN)
The First Booke of Songes or Ayres of foure parts. 1597.
The Second Booke of Songes or Ayres of 2, 4, and 5 parts. 1600.
The Third and Last Booke of Songs or Aires. 1603.
A Pilgrimes Solace, wherein is contained Musicall Harmonie of 3, 4, and 5 parts. 1612.

CAVENDISH (MICHAEL)
Ayres for four Voyces. 1599.

PILKINGTON (FRANCIS)
The First Booke of Songes or Ayres of 4 parts. 1605.

BARTLET (JOHN)
A Booke of Ayres with a Triplicitie of Musicke. 1606.

FORD (THOMAS)
Musicke of Sundrie Kindes, set forth in Two Bookes. 1607.

JONES (ROBERT)
Ultimum Vale, or the Third Book of Ayres of 1, 2, and 4 voyces.
A Musical Dreame or the Fourth Booke of Ayres. 1609.

CAMPION (THOMAS)
Two Bookes of Ayres. 1613.

N.B.—A number of the Songs contained in the above have been reprinted from time to time, and may be found in various present-day publishers' catalogues.

*The following separate Madrigals, selected from the foregoing Music
Books and edited by Charles Kennedy Scott, are published by the
Oxford University Press under the title of*

EUTERPE

BARTLET (JOHN)
1 *All my wits hath will enwrapped* (Ayre) (S.A.T.B.).
3*d.*

BATESON (THOMAS)
2 *Down the hills Corinna trips* (Madrigal)
(S.S.A.T.B.). 6*d.*
3 *I heard a noise* (Madrigal) (S.S.A.T.B.). 6*d.*

BENNET (JOHN)
61 *I languish to complain me* (Madrigal)
(S.A.T.B.).

BYRD (WILLIAM)
4 *Come, let us rejoice* (Psalm) (S.S.A.T.). 6*d.*
5 *This sweet and merry month of May* (Madrigal)
(S.S.A.T.T.B.). 6*d.*
6 *Let not the sluggish sleep* (S.A.T.B.). 4*d.*

CAMPION (THOMAS)
7 Three Ayres :
(a) *How eas'ly wert thou chained* (S.T.B.) ; (b) *O
what unhop'd for sweet supply* (S.A.B.) ; (c) *Where
she her sacred bow'r adorns* (S.T.B.). 4*d.*
8 Two Ayres :
(a) *Tune thy music to thy heart* (S.A.T.B.); (b) *O,
dear, that I with thee might live!* (S.T.B.). 4*d.*
9 *Out of my soul's depths to Thee* (Ayre) (S.A.T.B.).
4*d.*
10 *Though your strangeness* (Ayre) (S., or A., T.B.).
3*d.*
11 *Jack and Joan they think no ill* (Ayre) (S.T.B.).
3*d.*

DOWLAND (JOHN)
12 *Flow, my tears* (Ayre) (S., or T., B.). 4*d.*
13 *If my complaints* (Ayre) (S.A.T.B.). 6*d.*
14 *Me, me, and none but me* (Ayre) (S.A.T.B.). 3*d.*
15 *Fine knacks for ladies* (Ayre) (S.A.T.B.). 3*d.*
16 *Weep you no more, sad fountains!* (Ayre)
(S.A.T.B.). 3*d.*

17 *Sweet, stay awhile!* (Ayre) (S.A.T.B.). 3*d.*
18 *Disdain me still* (Ayre) (S.A.T.B.). 4*d.*
19 *Shall I strive with words to move?* (Ayre)
(S.A.T.B.). 4*d.*
20 *Come away, come, sweet Love* (Ayre) (S.A.T.B.).
4*d.*
21 *Stay, Time, awhile thy flying* (Ayre) (S.A.T.B.).
3*d.*
22 *Woeful heart with grief oppressed* (Ayre)
(S.A.T.B.). 3*d.*

DOWLAND (ROBERT)
23 *Up, merry mates!* (Ayre) (S.A.T.B.). 4*d.*

EAST (MICHAEL)
60 *Thyrsis, sleepest thou* (Madrigal) (S.S.A.T.
or A.).

FORD (THOMAS)
24 *What then is love, sings Coridon* (Ayre)
(S.A.T.B.) 4*d.*

GIBBONS (ORLANDO)
25 *Now each flow'ry bank* (Madrigal) (S.A.T.T.B.).
6*d.*

JONES (ROBERT)
26 *Though your strangeness* (Ayre) (S.A. or T.B.).
3*d.*

LICHFIELD (HENRY)
27 *I always lov'd to call my Lady 'Rose'* (Madrigal)
(S.S.A.T.B.). 6*d.*

MORLEY (THOMAS)
28 *Hark! Alleluia* (Ayre) (S.A.A.T.T.B.). 5*d.*
29 *Clorinda false, adieu!* (Madrigal) (S.A.T.B.).
6*d.*
30 Two Canzonets :
(a) *Fire and lightning from Heav'n* (T.T. or S.S.),
(b) *Flora, wilt thou torment me* (T.T.). 3*d.*
31 *Hark, jolly shepherds!* (Madrigal) (S.S.A.T.).
5*d.*

MUNDY (JOHN)

32 *Hear my prayer, O Lord* (Psalm) (S.T.B.). 3*d.*

33 *Sing ye unto the Lord* (Psalm) (S.S.A.T.). 4*d.*

34 *Hey ho! chill go to plough no more* (Secular Song) (S.S.A.B.). 5*d.*

59 *In deep distress* (Madrigal) (S.A.T.B.) 5*d.*

63 *In midst of woods* (Madrigal à 5). The first part.

64 *The blackbird made* (Madrigal à 5). The second part.

PHILIPS (PETER)

35 *The Nightingale* (Madrigal) (S.A.T.T.B.). 6*d.*

PILKINGTON (FRANCIS)

36 *The Messenger of the delightful Spring* (Madrigal) (S.A.T.B.). 5*d.*

37 *Sweet Phillida!* (Madrigal) (S.S.A.T.B.). 6*d.*

38 *Have I found her* (Madrigal) (S.A.T.B.). 4*d.*

62 *O softly singing lute* (Madrigal) (S.S.A.A.T.B.).

RAVENSCROFT (THOMAS)

39 (a) *We be Soldiers Three* (T.T.B.); (b) *We be Three Poor Mariners* (from Deuteromelia) (T.T.B.). 3*d.*

40 *Willy, prithee go to bed* (from Deuteromelia) (S.A.T.B.). 3*d.*

41 *To-morrow the Fox will come to Town* (from Deuteromelia) (S.A.T.B.). 4*d.*

42 *It was the Frog in the Well* (from Melismata) (S.A.T.B.). 3*d.*

43 *There were three Ravens* (from Melismata) (S.A.T.B.). 3*d.*

44 *A Wooing Song of a Yeoman of Kent's Son* (from Melismata) (S.A.T.B.). 3*d.*

ROSSETER (PHILIP)

55 Eight Solo Songs from *Book of Ayres.* 1*s.*

VAUTOR (THOMAS)

45 *Mother, I will have a husband* (Madrigal) (S.S.A.T.B.). 6*d.*

46 *Sweet Suffolk Owl* (Madrigal) (S.S.A.T.B.). 5*d.*

WEELKES (THOMAS)

47 *Cease, Sorrows, now* (Madrigal) (S.A.T.). 4*d.*

48 *When Thoralis delights to walk* (Madrigal) (S.S.A.T.T.B.). 6*d.*

49 *Those spots upon my Lady's face* (Madrigal) (S.S.A.T.T.B.). 4*d.*

57 *What have the Gods* (Madrigal) (S.S.A.A.T.B.). The first part. 6*d.*

58 *Methinks I hear* (Madrigal) (S.S.A.A.T.B.). The second part. 5*d.*

WHYTE (ROBERT)

50 *O praise God in His holiness* (Psalm) (S.A.T.B.). 6*d.*

WILBYE (JOHN)

51 *Happy, oh, happy he* (Madrigal) (S.A.T.B.). 6*d.*

52 *Fly not so swift, my dear* (Madrigal) (S.A.T.B.). 6*d.*

53 *Happy streams! whose trembling fall* (Madrigal) (S.S.A.T.). 6*d.*

YOULL (HENRY)

54 *Pipe, shepherds, pipe!* (Canzonet) (S.S.T.). 3*d.*

56 *The* EUTERPE *Round Book.* 1*s.* 6*d.*

The above represent choice specimens of the style. The series will be continued.